It CAN'T Be TRUE!

Senior editor Rob Houston
Editors Helen Abramson, Wendy Horobin,
Steve Setford, Rona Skene
Designers David Ball, Peter Laws,
Clare Marshall, Anis Sayyed, Jemma Westing
Illustrators Adam Benton, Stuart Jackson-Carter,
Anders Kjellberg, Simon Mumford
Creative retouching Steve Willis
Picture research Aditya Katyal, Martin Copeland

Jacket design Jessica Bentall,
Laura Brim, Jemma Westing
Jacket editor Manisha Majithia
Jacket design development manager
Sophia M Tampakopoulos Turner
Producer (pre-production) Rebekah Parsons-King
Production controller Mandy Inness

Managing art editor Philip Letsu
Managing editor Gareth Jones
Publisher Andrew Macintyre
Art director Phil Ormerod
Associate publishing director Liz Wheeler
Publishing director Jonathan Metcalf

Special sales & custom publishing manager
Michelle Baxter

This revised edition published in 2016
First published in Great Britain in 2013
by Dorling Kindersley Limited
80 Strand, London WC2R 0RL
Copyright © 2013, 2016 Dorling Kindersley Limited
A Penguin Company

10 9 8 7 6 5 4 3 2 1
001–192762–Oct/2017

ISBN: 978-0-2413-2714-2

Printed and bound in China

A WORLD OF IDEAS;
SEE ALL THERE IS TO KNOW
www.dk.com

CONTENTS

Out of this world

Astounding Earth

Humans and other life forms

Feats of engineering

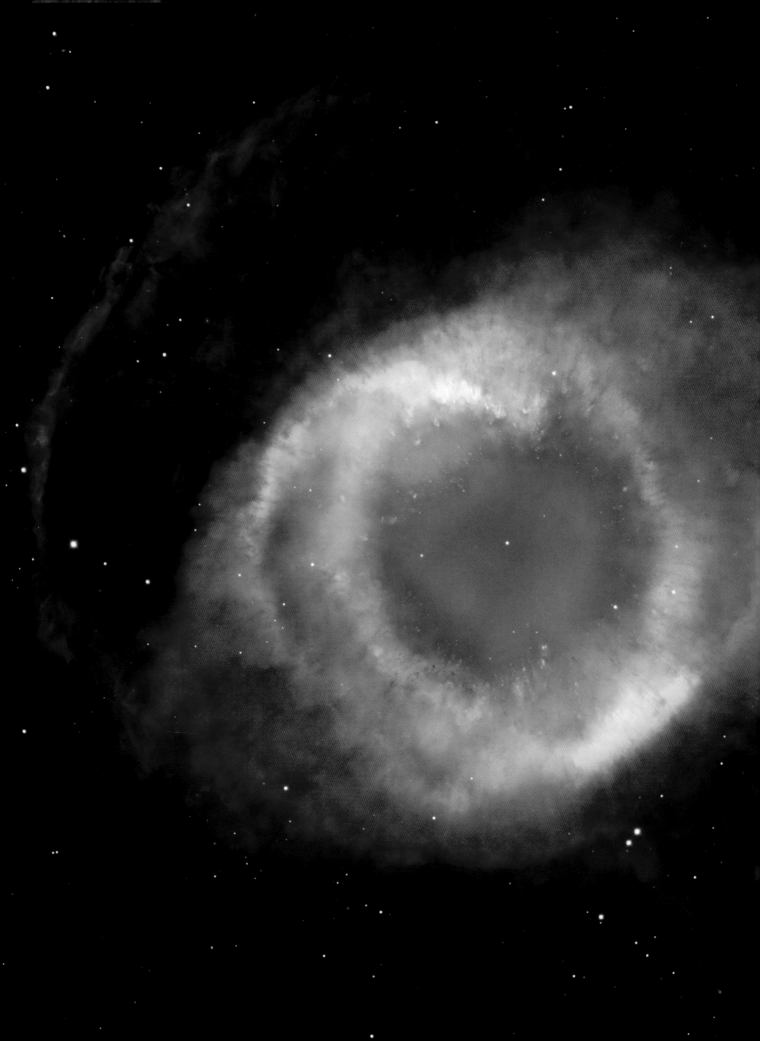

Out of this world

Beyond the safety of planet Earth, space is an incredibly hostile place – vast, airless, and unimaginably cold. But space is also full of amazing things, from fiery stars and weird worlds to mysterious moons, blazing comets, and hurtling asteroids.

The Helix Nebula is made up of huge shells of gas and dust thrown off by a dying star. It is expanding at a rate of nearly 115,000 kph (72,000 miles), which is around 10 times the speed of the fastest-ever aircraft, the rocket-powered North American X-15.

How **big** is the **Sun?**

The average **diameter** of the **Sun** is **1,391,016 km** (864,337 miles). It is more than **333,000 times** the mass of **Earth.**

You could fit **109 Earths** across the **diameter** of the Sun.

SUNSPOTS

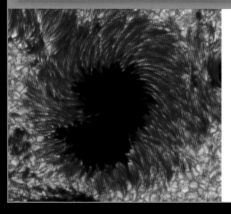

Sunspots are areas where a strong magnetic field stops hot gas reaching the surface. When sunspot numbers increase every 11 years, the Sun's intense magnetic activity can affect radio signals on Earth.

Sunspots are cooler patches on the Sun's surface. This one is a small one, but you could fit more than 15 Earths inside the largest spots.

Solar flares are eruptions that typically reach 100,000 km (62,000 miles) into space. About eight Earths would fit along one of these flares.

Sun

It takes about 225 million years for the Sun to orbit around the centre of the Milky Way. The Sun has made this journey 20 times since it formed around 4.6 billion years ago.

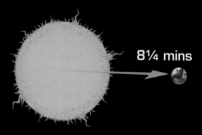

8¼ mins

Light takes about 8¼ minutes to travel from the surface of the Sun to Earth, 43 minutes to get to Jupiter, and around 4¼ hours to reach Neptune.

The grainy texture of the Sun is due to millions of columns of hot gas rising and falling

How **big** is the **Moon?**

The **Moon's diameter** is **3,475 km** (2,159 miles), **one-quarter** the size of **Earth's.** Its surface area is **13 times smaller.**

The Copernicus Crater, one of the Moon's largest, measures 93 km (58 miles) across.

A PERFECT FIT

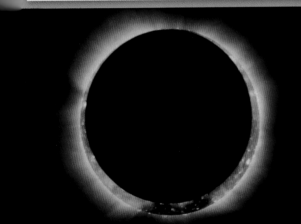

The Sun is 400 times the diameter of the Moon, but by an amazing coincidence, it is also 400 times further from Earth. This means that seen from Earth during an eclipse, the Sun and the Moon appear exactly the same size.

Australia

The Moon is the fifth-largest satellite in the Solar System, after three of Jupiter's moons and one of Saturn's. It is the Solar System's largest satellite relative to its planet. It doesn't usually hover above Australia, but orbits at a much more distant 384,399 km (238,854 miles) from Earth.

The Sea of Tranquility is a flat plain of lava that solidified around 4 billion years ago. It is a little larger than the British Isles.

The Moon is almost as wide as Australia, which is 3,983 km (2,475 miles) across at its widest point.

FAST FACTS

Earth measures 12,756 km (7,926 miles) across at the equator. Four Moons could line up across it.

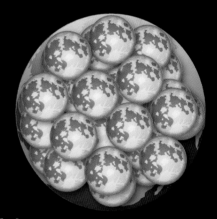

If there were no gaps, 50 Moons could fit inside the globe.

It would take 80 Moons to balance the scales against one Earth. Earth is so much heavier because its core is solid iron and as wide as two moons.

How big are the planets?

The **planets** in our Solar System **vary in size.** Some are **small and rocky**, while others are **enormous balls of gas.**

Venus is almost the same size and mass as Earth but is very different. Venus has a thick, poisonous atmosphere and a surface temperature of 464°C (867°F), which is hot enough to melt lead.

Jupiter, the biggest planet, measures 139,833 km (86,888 miles) across. It is made mainly of clouds of swirling gas.

Earth is 12,742 km (7,918 miles) in diameter on average, although like most planets, it is slightly fatter around the equator. It is the largest of the rocky planets.

⊞ FAST FACTS

Venus and Uranus spin in the opposite direction to the other planets. Uranus also rotates on its side, so it appears to spin clockwise or anticlockwise depending upon which pole you're looking at.

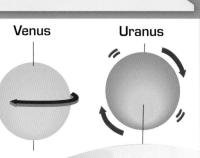

Venus   Uranus

Saturn is the second biggest planet at 116,464 km (72,367 miles) in diameter. It is made mainly of the gases hydrogen and helium.

Saturn's rings are made up of dust, rock, and ice. They extend 280,000 km (174,000 miles), but are only about 1 km (0.6 miles) thick.

Uranus is 50,724 km (31,518 miles) in diameter and is the furthest planet you can see with the naked eye. It is mostly made of gas, but possibly has an icy core.

Neptune is made of very cold gas. The furthest planet from the Sun, it has a diameter of 49,244 km (30,598 miles).

Venus is a rocky planet and, at 12,104 km (7,521 miles) across, is nearly as big as Earth.

Mars measures 6,799 km (4,225 miles) across. It is known as the "red planet" because of the colour of its rusty, iron-rich rocks.

Mercury is the smallest planet, just 4,879 km (3,032 miles) across. It lies the closest to the Sun and is made of rock.

Mercury is 29 times smaller around its equator than **Jupiter**.

How **big** are the **planets'** moons?

The **Solar System's** two **largest moons** are more than **5,000 km** (3,100 miles) across.

Titan is the only place in the Solar System other than Earth to have lakes – although they are filled with liquid methane and ethane.

Titan
5,150 km
(3,200 miles)

Our **Moon** is the fifth largest after Jupiter's **Ganymede, Callisto,** and **Io** and Saturn's **Titan.**

SATURN

Rhea
1,529 km
(950 miles)

Iapetus
1,471 km
(914 miles)

Dione
1,123 km
(698 miles)

Tethys
1,066 km
(662 miles)

Enceladus
504 km
(313 miles)

Mimas
396 km (246 miles)

The Moon
3,475 km (2,159 miles)

EARTH

📊 FAST FACTS

So far, 67 moons have been discovered around Jupiter – the most of any planet. Saturn is second with 62. Uranus has 27 moons, Neptune has 13, Mars has two, and Earth has just one. Venus and Mercury have none.

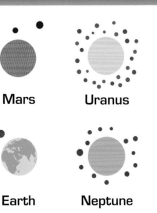

Mars

Uranus

Saturn

Earth

Neptune

Jupiter

Ganymede is the largest moon in the Solar System – it is bigger than Mercury and three quarters the size of Mars.

Ganymede
5,262 km
(3,270 miles)

HYPERION

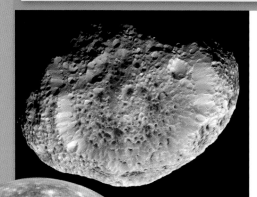

Larger moons usually have enough gravity to pull their material into a sphere, or ball shape. Saturn's small moon Hyperion does not have enough gravity, and so its shape is more like a potato.

Callisto
4,821 km
(2,995 miles)

Triton
2,707 km
(1,682 miles)

Europa
3,122 km
(1,940 miles)

NEPTUNE

Io
3,643 km
(2,264 miles)

JUPITER

Titania
1,578 km
(980 miles)

Oberon
1,523 km
(946 miles)

Both of Mars's tiny moons are possibly ex-asteroids, captured by Mars from the nearby asteroid belt.

Deimos
12 km (8 miles)

Phobos
22 km (14 miles)

MARS

Ariel
1,158 km
(726 miles)

Umbriel
1,169 km
(727 miles)

Miranda
472 km
(293 miles)

URANUS

There are 172 moons orbiting the major planets in the Solar System, although new ones are being discovered all the time. Pictured here are each of the planets' major moons. Moons also orbit some dwarf planets, such as Pluto, and even some asteroids.

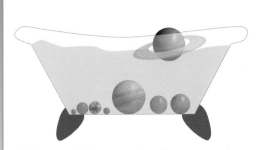

Although Saturn is the second biggest planet, it is not very dense. If you could fill with water a bathtub big enough, Saturn would float. All the other planets, including Jupiter, would sink to the bottom.

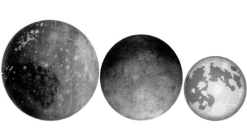

| Ganymede | Mercury | Moon |

Jupiter has at least 67 moons. The biggest, Ganymede, is also the largest moon in the Solar System. It is bigger than the planet Mercury and our own Moon.

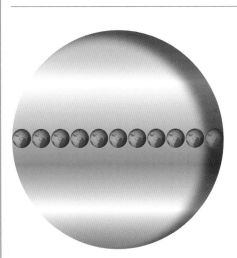

Around 11 Earths would fit across Jupiter's diameter.

Jupiter is made largely of gas, with a small rocky core. It is around two and a half times the combined mass of all the other planets put together.

Bands of cloud are created as Jupiter spins. It rotates once every 10 hours, faster than all the other planets.

How **big** is **Jupiter?**

More than 1,320 Earths would fit inside **Jupiter**.

The **biggest planet** in the Solar System is **Jupiter.** It has a **diameter** of **139,833 km** (86,888 miles), a **circumference** of **439,298 km** (272,967 miles) and its total **volume** is **1,431 trillion cu km** (343 trillion cu miles).

GREAT RED SPOT

The Great Red Spot is an enormous storm raging in the atmosphere of Jupiter. It is more than 20,000 km (12,000 miles) wide. You could fit two or three Earths inside it.

How **big** is an **asteroid?**

This mountain **is** one of the tallest peaks in the Solar System.

Asteroids range from rocks a few **tens of metres** across to the giants **Vesta** (**573 km**, 356 miles, across) and **Ceres** (**950 km**, 590 miles across). **Ceres** is now also classed as a **dwarf planet.**

United States

CHELYABINSK METEOR

If an asteroid enters Earth's atmosphere, it is called a meteor. In 2013, a meteor about 17 m (56 ft) wide exploded over Russia, shattering windows and damaging buildings with its shockwave.

The chances of something the size of Vesta being on a collision course with Earth are very slim. If it did hit our planet, the impact would be so catastrophic that no life would survive. The asteroid that killed the dinosaurs 65 million years ago was no more than 15 km (9 miles) across.

The surface of Vesta was studied in detail when the *Dawn* spacecraft spent a year orbiting the asteroid in 2011. Dawn revealed the surface to be covered in grooves and craters.

..... This row of three big craters has been nicknamed the "snowman craters". Here, the snowman's head is facing downwards.

Vesta is as wide as the entire Florida peninsula is long.

Florida

The Bahamas

FAST FACTS

1 Ceres 2 Pallas 3 Juno 4 Vesta 5 Astraea 6 Hebe 7 Iris 8 Flora 9 Metis 10 Hygiea

The Moon

The first 10 asteroids to be discovered were given the numbers 1–10 as part of their name. Even the biggest, Ceres, is much smaller than the Moon.

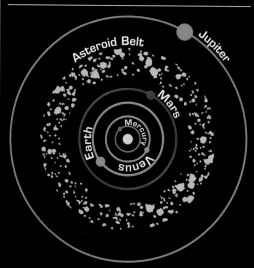

Asteroid Belt   Jupiter

Mars

Mercury

Earth   Venus

The Asteroid Belt between Jupiter and Mars contains millions of different-sized asteroids orbiting the Sun.

Dactyl 1.4 km (4,600 ft) across

Ida 54 km (33 miles) long

Some asteroids have moons. In 1994, for instance, scientists discovered that the asteroid Ida had a small moon, which they named Dactyl.

How big is a comet?

A comet's **nucleus** is **small**, but the **dust** and **gases** that surround it (the **coma**) can measure **100,000 km** (60,000 miles) across. Amazingly, the **tail** can be many **millions of kilometres** long.

CRASH LANDING

Most comets go around the Sun, but some are captured by Jupiter's massive gravitational pull. In July 1994, comet Shoemaker-Levy 9 broke into pieces and the fragments slammed into Jupiter, leaving a line of dark spots where they hit its atmosphere.

Jupiter
139,833 km
(86,888 miles) across

The tail is made of very thin, glowing gas. There is more matter in 1 cu mm of air than there is in 1 cu km (0.25 cu mile) of a comet's tail.

FAST FACTS

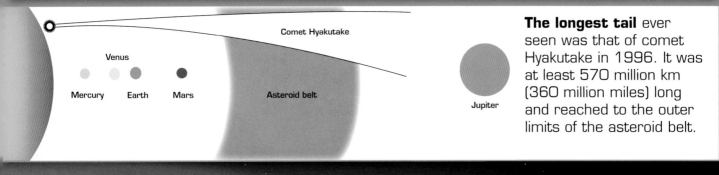

Mercury

Venus

Earth

Mars

Comet Hyakutake

Asteroid belt

Jupiter

The longest tail ever seen was that of comet Hyakutake in 1996. It was at least 570 million km (360 million miles) long and reached to the outer limits of the asteroid belt.

The nucleus of a comet usually measures less than **10 km (6 miles)** in diameter. However, it is surrounded by an enormous coma of dust and gases.

A comet's **coma** can spread nearly as wide as **Jupiter, the Solar System's** largest planet.

Comets spend most of their lives as small, icy bodies orbiting in the outer regions of the Solar System. The orbits of some comets, however, send them hurtling inwards. As a comet gets close to the Sun, its ice turns into gas and is blown away from the nucleus by the solar wind, forming a tail.

Where is the biggest canyon?

The **Valles Marineris** on **Mars** is up to **7 km** (4 miles) **deep** and more than **4,000 km** (2,500 miles) **long**. America's **Grand Canyon** would fit along its length **nine times**.

The deepest section of the canyon is the Melas Chasma. It is also the widest area at about 200 km (125 miles) across.

The **Valles Marineris** isn't a single valley, but a system of smaller canyons, or "chasmata".

4,000 km

GRAND CANYON SKYWALK

The Grand Canyon Skywalk is a transparent viewing platfom. Visitors can see through the walkway to the bottom of the canyon 1,200 m (4,000 ft) below.

If the **Valles Marineris** was in North America, it **would stretch** from the **Atlantic** to the **Pacific**.

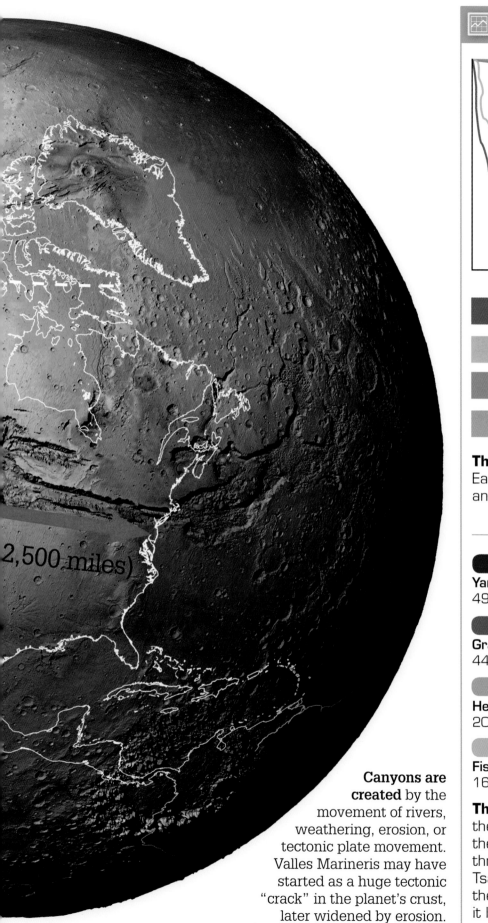

2,500 miles)

Canyons are created by the movement of rivers, weathering, erosion, or tectonic plate movement. Valles Marineris may have started as a huge tectonic "crack" in the planet's crust, later widened by erosion.

FAST FACTS

0 m
1,000 m (3,280 ft)
2,000 m (6,560 ft)
3,000 m (9,840 ft)
4,000 m (13,120 ft)
5,000 m (16,400 ft)
6,000 m (19,680 ft)
7,000 m (22,970 ft)
8,000 m (26,247 ft)

Valles Marineris (Mars)
7,000 m (22,965 ft)

Yarlung Tsangpo (Tibet, China)
6,009 m (19,685 ft)

Colca Canyon (Peru)
4,160 m (13,650 ft)

Grand Canyon (USA)
1,600 m (5,249 ft)

The deepest known canyons on Earth are the Yarlung Tsangpo and the Kali Gandaki (in Nepal).

Yarlung Tsangpo (Tibet, China)
496 km (308 miles)

Grand Canyon (USA)
445 km (277 miles)

Hell's Canyon (USA)
201 km (125 miles)

Fish River Canyon (Namibia)
160 km (100 miles)

The longest canyon on Earth, the Yarlung Tsangpo, is also the world's biggest. It was cut through Tibet by the Yarlung Tsangpo river, which becomes the Brahmaputra river when it later flows through India.

Solar System data

How long would it take a plane travelling at 900 kph (560 mph) to **reach each planet** from the Sun?

THE SIZE
OF THE SOLAR SYSTEM is equal to

100,000
times the distance from the Sun to Earth.

Travelling at 299,792 km per second (186,282 miles per second), sunlight takes

8¼ minutes
to reach Earth from the Sun, and **555.5 days** to reach the edge of the Solar System.

A **LONG** DAY
Because Mercury spins very slowly and orbits so close to the Sun, its day (measuring 176 Earth days), is actually

longer
than its year, which lasts for 87.87 Earth days.

COMETS
The nucleus of a comet can range in size from

100 m to 40 km
(300 ft to 25 miles)

Comets formed at the same time as the rest of Solar System, around

4.5
billion years ago. Like the planets, comets orbit the Sun.

When a comet gets near the Sun, its nucleus begins to melt, forming a **tail** of gas and dust that can

stre tch
for **millions of kilometres**.

MERCURY — 7.4 years

VENUS — 13.7 years

EARTH — 18.9 years

MARS — 28.9 years

JUPITER — 98.7 years

SATURN — 180.9 years

URANUS — 364.1 years

NEPTUNE — 570.5 years

DAY LENGTH
A **day** is measured as the **time** it takes for a planet to **spin once on its axis** so that the Sun returns to the same spot in the sky.

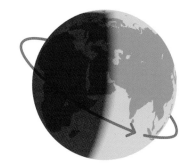

Mercury: 176 Earth days
Venus: 117 Earth days
Mars: 24 hr 40 min
Jupiter: 9 hr 56 min
Saturn: 10 hr 33 min
Uranus: 17 hr 14 min
Neptune: 16 hr 6 min

This list measures day length in Earth days, hours, and minutes.

DEEP PROBES

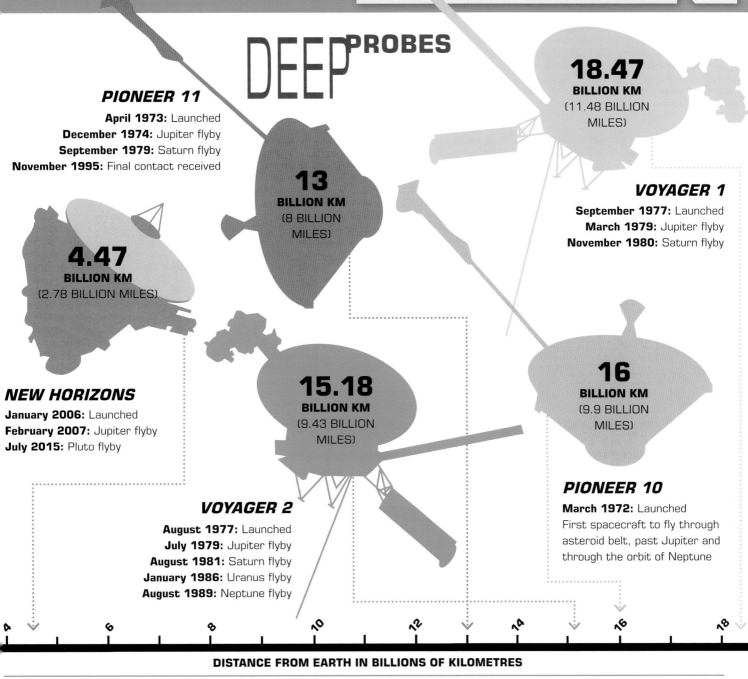

18.47 BILLION KM
(11.48 BILLION MILES)

13 BILLION KM
(8 BILLION MILES)

4.47 BILLION KM
(2.78 BILLION MILES)

15.18 BILLION KM
(9.43 BILLION MILES)

16 BILLION KM
(9.9 BILLION MILES)

PIONEER 11
April 1973: Launched
December 1974: Jupiter flyby
September 1979: Saturn flyby
November 1995: Final contact received

VOYAGER 1
September 1977: Launched
March 1979: Jupiter flyby
November 1980: Saturn flyby

NEW HORIZONS
January 2006: Launched
February 2007: Jupiter flyby
July 2015: Pluto flyby

VOYAGER 2
August 1977: Launched
July 1979: Jupiter flyby
August 1981: Saturn flyby
January 1986: Uranus flyby
August 1989: Neptune flyby

PIONEER 10
March 1972: Launched
First spacecraft to fly through asteroid belt, past Jupiter and through the orbit of Neptune

4 6 8 10 12 14 16 18

DISTANCE FROM EARTH IN BILLIONS OF KILOMETRES

DWARF PLANETS

As well as the eight large planets, the Solar System is also home to a number of smaller objects known as **dwarf planets**. The biggest discovered so far are:

Eris: radius 1,163 km (723 miles)

Pluto: radius 1,151 km (715 miles)

Makemake: radius 710 km (441 miles)

EXOPLANETS

Ours is not the only solar system. Other stars are also orbited by large satellites known as **exoplanets**.

The exoplanet **HAT-p-32b** is 1,044 light years from Earth and orbits a Sun-like star. Its **radius** is twice that of Jupiter. However, its **mass** is slightly less than that of Jupiter.

The exoplanet **KOI-55.01**, 3,850 light years from Earth, is **11 times** denser than Earth. It orbits its star, which is one-fifth the size of the Sun, every 5.8 hours – the **shortest orbit** of any known planet.

How big is the biggest star?

Hypergiant stars can be **hundreds of times** wider than the **Sun**. The **largest known star** is called **VY Canis Majoris**, whose diameter is nearly **2 billion km** (1.3 billion miles).

VY Canis Majoris's diameter is about **1,400 times bigger** than the **Sun's**.

FAST FACTS

If it were in the centre of our Solar System, VY Canis Majoris would engulf all the inner, rocky planets, including Earth. It would even swallow Jupiter, so the innermost surviving planet would be Saturn! When our own Sun begins to die in 5 billion years, it will swell to become a red giant, growing beyond the present orbit of Earth.

Saturn

Jupiter

Mars

Earth

VY Canis Majoris

Sun

Aldebaran is a red giant star 67 light years away and 44 times wider than the Sun.

Arcturus is a red giant 37 light years away and 25 times wider than the Sun. It is the fourth-brightest star in the night sky.

When compared with giant, supergiant, and hypergiant stars, our own Sun appears tiny.

Sun

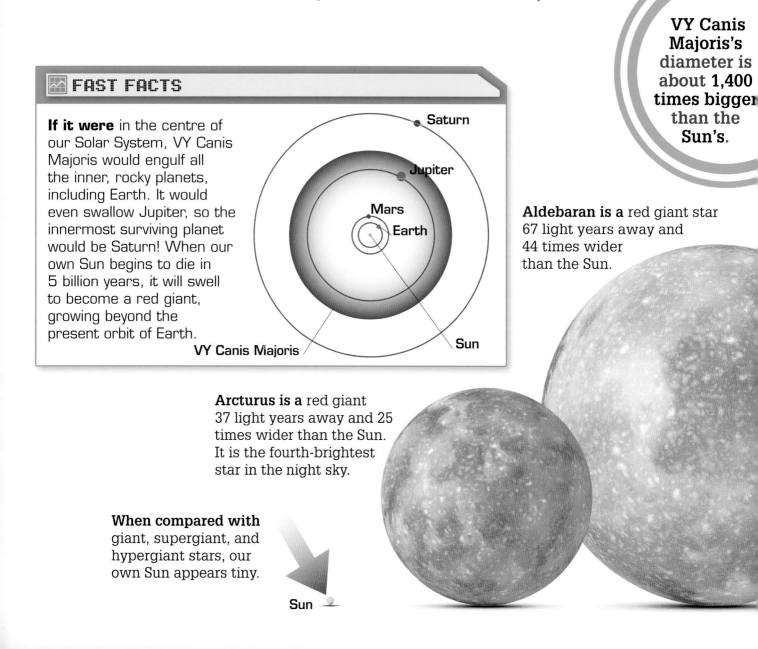

SUPERNOVA

When large red giants die, their cores may collapse under their great gravity, then may explode with incredible force. These explosions are called supernovas, and they blow a star's matter into space as a cloud of dust and gas called a nebula. This one is the Crab Nebula, and it comes from a star that exploded like this in 1054 CE.

VY Canis Majoris is a red hypergiant about 4,000 light years away. It is 1,400 times wider than the Sun, but only 20–30 times heavier. Its outer layers are very thin – 1,000 times thinner than Earth's atmosphere. VY Canis Majoris is burning very brightly, producing about 500,000 times as much light as the Sun. The force of its burning is pushing its thin outer layers out into space.

Rigel is a blue-white supergiant 860 light years away and around 75 times wider than the Sun. In spite of its distance from Earth, it is so luminous that it is still one of the brightest stars in our sky.

Neutron stars are among the most extreme places in the Universe. Their temperature is more than 1 million °C (1.8 million °F) and some spin hundreds of times a second. Gravity on their surface is around 200 billion times stronger than on Earth.

Neutron stars appear a dim blue-white colour. Because they are so hot, they give off little visible light. Instead, they shine with more powerful X-rays.

FAST FACTS

A neutron star is the core of a giant star that has collapsed under its own gravity. The collapse squeezes the neutron star's matter into a minute space.

Earth ● Neutron star

Neutron stars shrink so much when they collapse that they pack a mass greater than the Sun into a sphere less than 30 km (19 miles) in diameter – about the size of a city. A neutron star's diameter is 425 times smaller than Earth's.

What is the heaviest stuff in the Universe?

The **matter** in a **neutron star** is so dense that a piece the size of **sugar cube** weighs the same as all the **humans** on **Earth.**

PULSING STAR

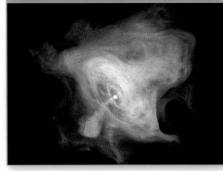

In the centre of this whirling disc of hot matter is a neutron star blasting out a beam of radiation and a plume of hot gas. Thirty times every second, the beam points towards Earth, giving viewers a pulse of light.

A pinhead has a volume of around 1 cu mm. The matter in a neutron star is so dense that a pinhead-sized piece would weigh 1 million tonnes (1.1 million tons).

Pinhead-sized piece of neutron star material

A pinhead-sized blob of matter from a neutron star is as heavy as three Empire State Buildings.

The Empire State Building weighs 331,000 tonnes (365,000 tons), so three would weigh 993,000 tonnes (1,095,000 tons).

How **fast** is **light?**

It may seem to move instantly, but **light** takes time to get from place to place. In space, **light travels** at **1,080,000,000 kph** (671 million mph), or **299,792 km** (186,282 miles) in **1 second**.

00:00

An imaginary light beam begins its journey.

Stopwatch reads
0 seconds

📈 FAST FACTS

Vacuum 100% speed

Air 99.97% speed

Water 75% speed

Glass 65% speed

Light travels at a constant speed in a vacuum, but it slows down when there are particles in the way. In air, it travels at 99.97 per cent of its speed in a vacuum, in water 75 per cent, and in glass about 65 per cent.

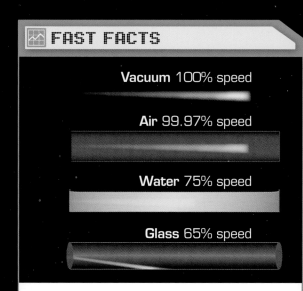

This picture shows light bending, but in reality, light only curves sharply like this when pulled by really intense gravity, such as that generated by a black hole. Earth's gravity is too weak to make much difference to light's straight-line path.

In just **1 second**, a beam of **light** would travel around **Earth** 7.5 times.

LUNAR LASER

A laser beam, travelling at the speed of light, takes 1.28 seconds to reach the Moon. From this, we can precisely measure the distance from Earth to the Moon: 384,399 km (238,854 miles).

The light beam completes its 1-second journey more than 18,000 times quicker than the fastest-ever spacecraft – the *New Horizons* probe, which reached 58,536 kph (36,373 mph) as it left Earth's atmosphere in 2006.

Stopwatch reads 1 second

How big is the Universe?

The Universe is unimaginably vast. Distances are so huge that scientists measure them in **light-years** – the distance that light travels in one year.

The Milky Way, a disc-shaped spiral galaxy, contains the Solar System. This galaxy is about 100,000 light-years across. One light-year is 9,461 billion km (5,879 billion miles).

FAST FACTS

ONE YEAR
J F M A
M J J A
S O N D
31

The Universe is 13.77 billion years old. Humans have not been around for that long. If the Universe were just a year old, *Homo sapiens* (humans) would only have emerged at 11:52 pm on New Year's Eve.

The Sun is about 150 million km (93 million miles) from planet Earth.

The Solar System contains the Sun and the objects orbiting around it, which include Earth, seven other planets, and many asteroids.

Our home, Earth, is a small planet measuring about 12,742 km (7,918 miles) across.

From top to bottom, South America stretches about 7,500 km (4,660 miles).

The orbit of Uranus, the Solar System's second most distant planet, lies on average 2.78 billion km (1.79 billion miles) from the Sun.

MILKY WAY

Although disc-shaped, the Milky Way appears in our skies as a bright band. That's because Earth (and all stars visible without a telescope) sits within the disc.

The Andromeda galaxy is a large galaxy in the Local Group, a cluster of nearly 46 galaxies.

The Local Group of galaxies takes up an area of space that is about 10 million light-years across. The Milky Way is a tiny part of the Local Group.

A supermassive black hole is thought to sit in the middle of the Milky Way. It contains as much mass as 4 million Suns.

The edge of the observable Universe is 13.7 billion light-years away.

This image taken by the Hubble Telescope shows galaxies up to 13.7 billion light-years away. However, the Universe has expanded since light left these galaxies, so they are now even further away.

The red dots are the most distant galaxies that we can see.

Astounding Earth

Our planet has been shaped by immense forces since it was formed – from volcanic eruptions and asteroids to the weather. Today, high mountains stretch skywards, canyons and caves plunge into Earth's depths, and vast rivers snake across the land.

Tourists at the Grand Canyon, Arizona, USA, marvel at the view – and the hair-rasing drop! The canyon is around 1.8 km (1 mile) deep – the height of four Empire State Buildings stacked one on top of the other.

Which is the biggest continent?

At **44,568,500 sq km (17,207,994 sq miles), Asia is the biggest** of the world's seven large landmasses, or **continents**.

Australasia has an area of 8,525,989 sq km (3,291,903 sq miles) and includes Australia, New Zealand, New Guinea, and some of the islands in between.

Greenland

New Guinea

Baffin Island (Canada)

Borneo   Madagascar

Islands are smaller landmasses surrounded by water. Greenland is the world's largest island at around 2,166,086 sq km (836,330 sq miles). It is more than double the size of the second largest island, New Guinea, which has an area of 785,753 sq km (303,380 sq miles).

Europe has an area of 9,948,000 sq km (3,840,944 sq miles) and covers only 7 per cent of the land surface and is only slightly bigger than Canada.

Antarctica covers an area of 14,000,000 sq km (5,405,430 sq miles). This landmass is almost entirely covered in ice.

A continent is usually a large mass of land that is separated from another by water. In fact, five of the seven continents are joined. Europe and Asia are sometimes considered as a single continent, Eurasia.

South American has an area of 17,819,000 sq km (6,879,954 sq miles). This continent stretches from just above the Equator down to the Antarctic.

North America covers 24,473,000 sq km (9,449,078 sq miles). Greenland is part of this continent, although it belongs to Denmark.

Africa has an area of 30,065,000 sq km (11,608,161 sq miles). It covers an area more than three times bigger than the USA.

Asia covers about 30 per cent of the Earth's land surface.

Asia is a huge continent, and is home to about 60 per cent of the world's population.

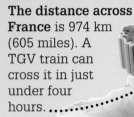

The distance across France is 974 km (605 miles). A TGV train can cross it in just under four hours.

The distance across Algeria is 2,400 km (1,500 miles). Travel can be tricky due to sand dunes forming on roads in the Sahara.

The distance across Australia is 3,983 km (2,475 miles). The train journey from east to west passes along the world's longest stretch of straight track, which measures 478 km (297 miles).

France

Algeria

Australia

USA

Russia

The distance across the USA is 4,517 km (2,807 miles). It would take about 2 months travelling 80 km (50 miles) per day to cycle across it.

The distance across Russia is 9,650 km (5,996 miles). The country is so wide that the eastern edge of the country is nine hours ahead of the west.

SMALLEST COUNTRY

The smallest country in the world is the Vatican City. It occupies 0.44 sq km (0.17 sq miles) within Rome, Italy. That is roughly the area of 65 football pitches. Fewer than 1,000 people live there.

What is the biggest country?

Russia stretches across **two continents** and covers **11.5 per cent** of **Earth's land surface.**

Russia

Russia is nearly **twice as wide** as the **US** (excluding Alaska) and nearly **10 times** as **wide** as France.

Vladivostok in Russia is at the eastern end of the Trans-Siberian railway, which crosses Russia from Moscow. The 9,289-km (5,772-mile) journey takes 6 days.

FAST FACTS

Africa contains more countries than any other continent.

Africa	54
Europe	47
Asia	44
North America	23
Australasia and Oceania	14
South America	12
Antarctica	0 (It belongs to no one.)

What is the biggest river?

Along much of its length, the Amazon is 1.6–10 km (1–6 miles) wide in the dry season. However, in the rainy season some parts expand to 48 km (30 miles) or more.

Although not as **long** as the **Nile**, the **Amazon** carries **far more water**. It empties **219 million litres** (58 million gallons) into the ocean every second – that's **one fifth** of all the **world's river water flow**.

Pará River

FAST FACTS

The Amazon Basin is the area drained by the Amazon River. It is almost as big as Australia and is the largest river basin in the world. It covers 40 per cent of South America, and all of it recieves heavy yearly rainfall, which swells the river with water.

The Pará River joins the Amazon at its mouth, broadening its estuary still further.

The Amazon spreads out when it reaches the Atlantic Ocean and merges with the mouth of another wide river, the Pará. This image shows the region around this mouth, or estuary – sometimes called "The Mouths of the Amazon".

More than 1,100 tributaries feed directly into the Amazon, 15 of which are themselves more than 1,000 km (620 miles) long.

FLOODED RAINFOREST

In the yearly rainy season, the Amazon River rises over 9 m (30 ft) and floods about 240,000 sq km (90,000 sq miles) of surrounding forest.

The Amazon Rainforest, the world's largest rainforest, surrounds the river. It covers much of Brazil and parts of eight other countries.

Amazon River

London to Paris 344 km (214 miles)

The Amazon flows with such force that it sends a plume of fresh water about 400 km (250 miles) into the Atlantic. It floats on the sea, so fresh water can be found on the surface even well out of sight of land.

The **mouth of the Amazon is nearly as wide as the** distance from **London to Paris.**

How high is the tallest waterfall?

The **tallest waterfall** in the world, **Angel Falls** in Venezuela, is **979 m** (3,212 ft) **in height**. Known locally as **Kerepakupai Merú**, it found fame when US pilot **Jimmy Angel** discovered it in 1933.

Vinnufossen, Norway
865 m (2,837 ft)

Sutherland Falls, New Zealand
580 m (1,903 ft)

Surtherland Falls drops down the almost sheer side of a fjord – a valley carved by a glacier and flooded by the sea.

Victoria Falls, Zambia/Zimbabwe
108 m (354 ft)

Niagara Falls, USA/Canada
51 m (167 ft)

The spray can be seen from 48 km (30 miles) away.

VICTORIA FALLS

Victoria Falls forms the largest continuous sheet of falling water in the world, at 1.7 km (1.1 mile) wide and 108 m (355 ft) tall.

**Angel Falls,
Venezuela**
979 m (3,212 ft)

📈 **FAST FACTS**

Niagara Falls

**Olympic
swimming pool**

Niagara Falls, on the US–Canadian border, is the world's largest waterfall in terms of water flow. In just 1 second, 2.8 million litres (740,000 gallons) of water gushes over the falls – enough to fill an Olympic swimming pool.

In 1901, Ann Taylor became the first person to go over Niagara Falls in a barrel and survive to tell the tale. Of the 14 other people who have intentionally gone over the falls since, five did not survive the experience.

Angel Falls is formed by water tumbling down the side of one of the "tepuis", Venezuela's vertical-sided mountains. Here, it is pictured next to some of the world's other tall and famous waterfalls.

The Empire State Building measures 443 m (1,453 ft) tall.

Angel Falls is more than twice as tall as New York's Empire State Building.

FAST FACTS

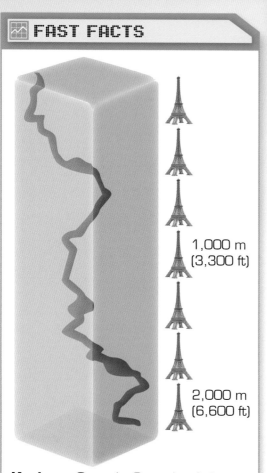

1,000 m
(3,300 ft)

2,000 m
(6,600 ft)

Krubera Cave in Georgia, Asia, is the world's deepest at 2,197 m (7,208 ft) – nearly as deep as seven Eiffel Towers.

An underground river runs through the first 2.5 km (1.5 miles) of the 9-km (5.5-mile) cave. There are thought to be more than 150 chambers in total.

How big is the biggest cave?

Deep in the **Vietnamese jungle** lies the **Hang Son Doong** cave – the **biggest** in the **world**. In places it is more than **200 m (650 ft) high.**

Each of the sinkholes on the surface is up to 100 m (330 ft) across.

Hang Son Doong cave was not discovered until 1991 because it was hidden by thick jungle. The cave formed between 2 and 5 million years ago, as underground river water eroded away the limestone rock. In places where the rock was weak, the ceiling collapsed into giant sinkholes.

Six Towers of Pisa would fit in the **deepest shaft** if stacked on top of one another.

ROCK PILLARS

Stalagmites in the cave, like the "Hand of Dog" shown here, are so big that they make the man standing in the middle look tiny.

The two main chambers within the cave system have 30-m (100-ft) trees growing inside because the roofs fell in and let in enough light for plants to grow.

This shows the upper slopes of Mount Everest. There are deep valleys around the mountain that are not visible here.

Aconcagua, Argentina
6,961 m (22,837 ft)

A mountain's height is usually given as its height above sea level. If you could strip away the land from the base of each mountain and place them together, this is what you would see in terms of height differences.

Mount McKinley, USA
6,194 m (20,320 ft)

Mount Kilimanjaro, Tanzania 5,895 m (19,341 ft)

Everest is 10 times taller than the world's tallest building, Dubai's **Burj Khalifa**.

Mount Everest, Nepal
8,848 m (29,029 ft)

Burj Khalifa, Dubai
828 m (2,717 ft)

Sea level

STILL GROWING

Mount Everest was formed by two tectonic plates (sections of Earth's crust) colliding. The two plates are still pushing together, so the mountain is growing by about 5 mm (0.25 in) every year.

How **high** is Mount Everest?

The peak of **Mount Everest,** the **highest mountain** in the world, is **8,848 m (29,029 ft)** above sea level.

Mount Elbrus, Russia
5,642 m (18,510 ft)

Vinson Massif, Antarctica
4,892 m (16,050 ft)

Mount Wilhelm, Papua New Guinea
4,509 m (14,793 ft)

These seven mountains are known as the "Seven Summits"; each is the highest mountain on its continent. Reaching the top of all of them has become a mountaineering challenge.

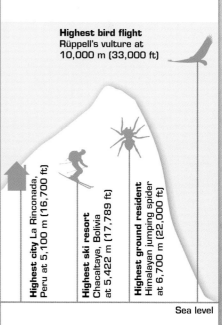

FAST FACTS

Olympus Mons

Mauna Kea

Everest

Everest is not Earth's tallest mountain. Measured from its base on the ocean floor, Mauna Kea, Hawaii, is taller. However, both are dwarfed by Olympus Mons on Mars, which is 22 km (14 miles) high.

Highest bird flight
Rüppell's vulture at 10,000 m (33,000 ft)

Highest city La Rinconada, Peru at 5,100 m (16,700 ft)

Highest ski resort Chacaltaya, Bolivia at 5,422 m (17,789 ft)

Highest ground resident Himalayan jumping spider at 6,700 m (22,000 ft)

Sea level

A small jumping spider on Everest is thought to be Earth's highest animal ground resident. In Africa, Rüppell's vulture can fly even higher.

The Australian, Arabian, and Sahara deserts are hot deserts in the tropics. The biggest is the Sahara in Africa, which is as big as the USA. The Kalahari and Gobi lie further from the Equator and can be cool or even very cold.

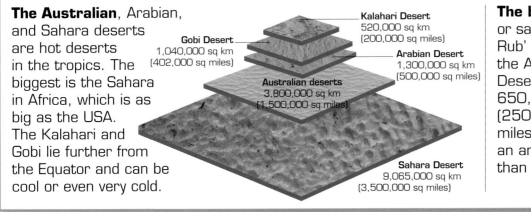

Gobi Desert
1,040,000 sq km
(402,000 sq miles)

Kalahari Desert
520,000 sq km
(200,000 sq miles)

Arabian Desert
1,300,000 sq km
(500,000 sq miles)

Australian deserts
3,800,000 sq km
(1,500,000 sq miles)

Sahara Desert
9,065,000 sq km
(3,500,000 sq miles)

The biggest erg, or sand sea, is the Rub' al Khali in the Arabian Desert. At 650,000 sq km (250,000 sq miles), it covers an area bigger than France.

France

How tall are sand dunes?

Trains of camels were the best method of transport in the Sahara for many centuries and are still sometimes used to carry goods across the desert.

Tall dunes often reach **450 m** (1,500 ft) in height, but occasionally, dunes **can** even **grow** to **1,200 m** (4,000 ft).

MARTIAN SAND DUNES

Near Mars's north pole is a field of dunes covered with frozen pink carbon dioxide in winter. In spring, dark sand trickles down the slopes as the carbon dioxide melts.

The peak is sculpted by winds blowing from many directions piling sand up into the centre.

Saharan trader with camel loaded with goods

Desert

Land

Sand dunes

One third of Earth's land surface is desert, but only 10 per cent of the deserts is sand dunes. The rest is rock, earth, and sheets of sand.

You could bury the Eiffel Tower inside a big Saharan star dune.

This Saharan star dune is 450 m (1,500 ft) tall. Star dunes are pyramid-shaped and they tend to form in areas without a dominant wind direction.

Dust devils are columns of dusty air heated by the Sun. They begin to spin as they rise through the cooler air above.

Great Pyramid
Original height
147 m (481 ft)

Eiffel Tower
324 m (1,063 ft)

How powerful was the Krakatoa volcano?

In **1883**, Krakatoa, a volcano in **Indonesia**, erupted with a force of about **200 megatons** of **TNT** explosive, or **several nuclear bombs**.

ASH CLOUD LIGHTNING

The electrical charge in the ash cloud from a volcanic eruption can cause lightning, as in the 2010 Eyjafjallajökull eruption in Iceland.

The ash cloud caused by the Krakatoa eruption rose to an estimated height of 80 km (50 miles).

Krakatoa was four times as powerful as the Tsar Bomba, the largest nuclear weapon ever detonated.

The mushroom cloud produced by the detonation of the Tsar Bomba rose to a height of 65 km (40 miles). The bomb was a nuclear weapon dropped over remote Siberian islands during tests by the Soviet Union in 1961.

Krakatoa produced one of the greatest volcanic eruptions in history. It destroyed more than two-thirds of Krakatoa island, killing more than 36,000 people. People reported hearing the explosion 4,500 km (2,800 miles) away.

FAST FACTS

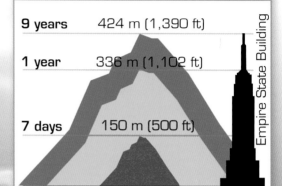

		Empire State Building
9 years	424 m (1,390 ft)	
1 year	336 m (1,102 ft)	
7 days	150 m (500 ft)	

A volcano in Parícutin, Mexico, suddenly erupted in 1943 from a cornfield. It grew 150 m (500 ft) in one week and continued to erupt and grow for another nine years.

Mt St Helen's 1 cu km (0.25 cu miles)

Krakatoa 18 cu km (4 cu miles)

Yellowstone 2,500 cu km (600 cu miles)

The Yellowstone supervolcano, 2.1 million years ago, produced 135 times more ash than Krakatoa and 2,500 times more than Mount St Helen's.

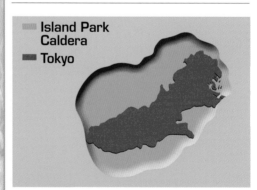

Island Park Caldera

Tokyo

Yellowstone's Island Park Caldera, an enormous volcanic crater, could fit a city of 13 million people, such as Tokyo, inside it.

What's the largest crater on Earth?

Asteroid and **comet** impacts make **craters** on **Earth** just like on the Moon. The **largest** one is the **Vredefort crater** in South Africa, which is over **300 km** (186 miles) **wide.**

You could fit **250 Barringer craters** into **Vredefort.**

Barringer crater is a well-preserved impact crater in Arizona, US. Its shape is so clear because it is only 50,000 years old.

Asteroids and comets have battered Earth over the course of its life, but we can see only a few clear craters on Earth's surface today. This is because most craters are worn down or buried under younger rock.

FAST FACTS

Herschel crater
central peak
6,500 m
(21,300 ft)

Mt. Everest
8,848 m
(29,029 ft)

Saturn's moon Mimas is marked by a huge crater, named Herschel, with a central peak made by the shockwave of the impact. The peak is nearly as tall as Mount Everest.

The Borealis Basin on Mars is thought to be the biggest known land feature caused by an impact. If it is, it must have been the result of a blow from an object the size of Pluto. The basin covers most of the northern half of Mars, and is nearly five times the size of the USA.

USA

Borealis
Basin

Barringer crater is only 1.2 km (³/₄ mile) in diameter.

Chicxulub crater in Mexico is 180 km (110 miles) wide. It was formed 65 million years ago by the impact of an object 10 km (6 miles) across hitting Earth. The destruction it caused is blamed for the death of the dinosaurs. The crater is now buried and half of it is hidden on the seabed.

Vredefort crater was made around 2 billion years ago. In all that time, it has been eroded by wind, rain, and rivers, and bent and distorted by movements in the Earth's crust.

BIGGEST METEORITE

When an object falls from space and survives the impact, it is known as a meteorite. The Hoba meteorite in Namibia is the biggest ever found and weighs more than 60 tons (66 tonnes).

How big are the biggest crystals?

Crystals of **selenite** discovered in a cave in **Mexico** measure up to **11.4 m (37.4 ft) long.**

With temperatures in the cave of 48°C (118°F) and 98 per cent humidity, people have to wear protective suits to explore the amazing crystals formations.

FAST FACTS

The longest Naica crystal found so far, Crystal Cin, is around the length of a bus and weighs about the same as 8 African elephants!

Crystal Cin

Length 11.4 m (37.4 ft)

Single decker bus

The oldest crystal in the cave dates back 600,000 years – about the time when *Homo heidelbergensis*, the ancestors of modern humans, first appeared.

Present day

600,000 years ago

These vast selenite crystals are in the Cave of Crystals, which lies 300 m (985 ft) below ground in a mine at Naica, northern Mexico. The crystals began to grow because of water boiling in this underground chamber. The water actually boiled for about 500,000 years, the heat solidifying the crystals in the water.

FINGAL'S CAVE

Fingal's Cave, off the coast of Scotland, is unique. It is formed from hexagonal pillars of basalt rock more than 20 m (65 ft) tall. They formed when an ancient lava flow cooled and cracked.

The **largest crystals** in the cave are more than **six times taller than a person**.

How much water is there?

The world contains **1.3 billion cu km** (332 million cu miles) of **water** in its oceans, rivers, lakes, groundwater, and clouds, and – as **ice** – in its glaciers and ice caps.

Scooped up, **the world's water** would **form a ball** just **1,384 km (860 miles) wide.**

ICE CAPS AND GLACIERS

Only 2.5 per cent of the world's water is fresh, and most of this fresh water is locked up in glaciers and ice caps. This leaves less than 1 per cent of Earth's water that is liquid and fresh.

This globe shows the ocean basins with all their water removed. Nearly 97 per cent of the world's water is in oceans. The next biggest store of water is the ice caps and glaciers, with 1.75 per cent.

Permafrost (underground ice) in Siberia locks up a lot of water. Permafrost and liquid groundwater (water in rocks and soil) make up 1.7 per cent of the world's total water.

FAST FACTS

Water 71%

Land 29%

More than two-thirds of the planet's surface is covered with water, leaving 29 per cent land.

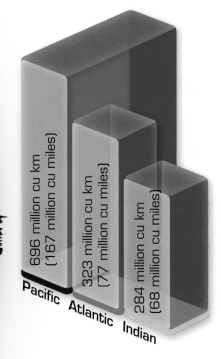

696 million cu km (167 million cu miles)

323 million cu km (77 million cu miles)

284 million cu km (68 million cu miles)

Pacific Atlantic Indian

The Pacific Ocean contains more water than all the world's other seas and oceans together.

For every bathful of sea water on Earth, there are just 4 teaspoons of fresh water in lakes, rivers, and the atmosphere.

When water fills this ocean basin, the sea bed is around 4,000 m (12,000 ft) below the surface.

How deep is the ocean?

The **average depth** of the ocean is 4,300 m (14,000 ft), but the **deepest point** is **11,030 m** (36,200 ft) below sea level at **Challenger Deep** in the Pacific Ocean.

Continental shelves are the shallow regions fringing deep oceans. They are actually part of the continental landmass. A shelf may extend hundreds of kilometres from the coast.

BARRELEYE

This barreleye, or spookfish, is one of the many peculiar creatures that inhabit the dark ocean depths. The Barreleye lives 600–800 m (2,000–2,600 ft) under water and has unique tube-shaped eyes inside a transparent head.

The Empire State Building measures 381 m (1,250 ft) to the top of its roof.

It would take 29 stacked Empire State Buildings to reach the bottom of Challenger Deep.

Continental shelf
Shoreline to 140 m (460 ft)

Continental slope
140–3,200 m
(460–10,500 ft)

Abyssal plain
3,200–6,000 m
(10,500–20,000 ft)

Ocean trench
6,000–11,030 m
(20,000–36,200 ft)

Challenger Deep
11,030 m (36,200 ft)

The sea bed is not flat. It starts with a gradual descent down the continental shelf where the land gives way to sea along the coast. It then plunges down the continental slope to the deep ocean floor, or abyssal plain. The sea bed has ridges or deep trenches, such as the Mariana Trench in the western Pacific – where Challenger Deep is located.

FAST FACTS

Unexplored ocean

Explored ocean

Humans have explored less than 10 per cent of the ocean. Fewer people have travelled to the deepest parts of the ocean than have gone into outer space.

Mount Everest

Mariana Trench

The Mariana Trench is about 11 km (7 miles) deep. If Mount Everest were put at the bottom of the trench, the peak would still be more than 2 km (1.2 miles) below sea level.

Cup before dive

Cup after dive

If a polystyrene cup were taken 3 km (1.9 miles) under water, the pressure at this depth would squeeze it to less than half of its original size.

How **tall** was the **biggest wave** ever **surfed?**

In 2013, American professional big-wave surfer **Garrett McNamara** surfed a **wave** that was **23.8 m** (78 ft) **tall** off the coast of Nazaré, Portugal.

📈 FAST FACTS

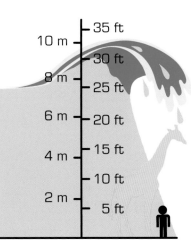

10 m	35 ft
8 m	30 ft
	25 ft
6 m	20 ft
4 m	15 ft
	10 ft
2 m	5 ft

Tsunamis tend to be less than 10 m (33 ft) tall, but because there is a lot of water following behind them, they cause a flood that reaches far inland. They are caused by earthquakes on the sea bed, land slips, and asteroid strikes.

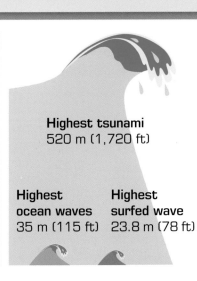

Highest tsunami
520 m (1,720 ft)

Highest ocean waves
35 m (115 ft)

Highest surfed wave
23.8 m (78 ft)

The biggest wave ever known occurred in Lituya Bay, Alaska, when a slab of rock slipped into the bay and caused a huge tsunami. Giant ocean waves also form far out at sea, caused by high winds and strong currents.

Foaming breakers rise up almost vertically before curling over to form a tube. The surfer tries to stay inside the tube and, if possible, reach the end of it before the wave collapses.

A **23.8-m (78-ft) wave** is the **height** of more than **13 people** standing on top of each other.

Surfboards come in a variety of sizes. This championship board is 2.1 m (7 ft) long.

TSUNAMI DAMAGE

Tsunamis are so powerful that anything in their way is flattened and swept away. Even large ships can be carried inland, leaving them stranded miles from the shore.

Record waves occur off Nazaré because it faces the huge swells caused by distant Atlantic storms. An undersea canyon then funnels the wave energy of the swells onto a short stretch of the coast, piling the waters high.

How big was the biggest iceberg?

The **biggest-ever** iceberg began its life when it broke free from an ice shelf off **Antarctica** in 1956. It was **335 km** (208 miles) **long** and **100 km** (60 miles) **wide.**

The biggest iceberg was not really shaped like Belgium. It was longer and thinner, but its area of 31,000 sq km (12,000 sq miles) was slightly larger than Belgium's. It was larger even than iceberg B-15 – the Jamaica-sized iceberg that broke off Antarctica's Ross Ice Shelf in 2000.

Antwerp

Bruges

Ghent

Brussels

B E L G

Flanders

HIDDEN DEPTHS

Icebergs float low in the water, with around 90 per cent of their height hidden beneath the waves. The ice below the water melts faster than that above it, so that an iceberg may suddenly roll over with a great crash that can be heard for miles.

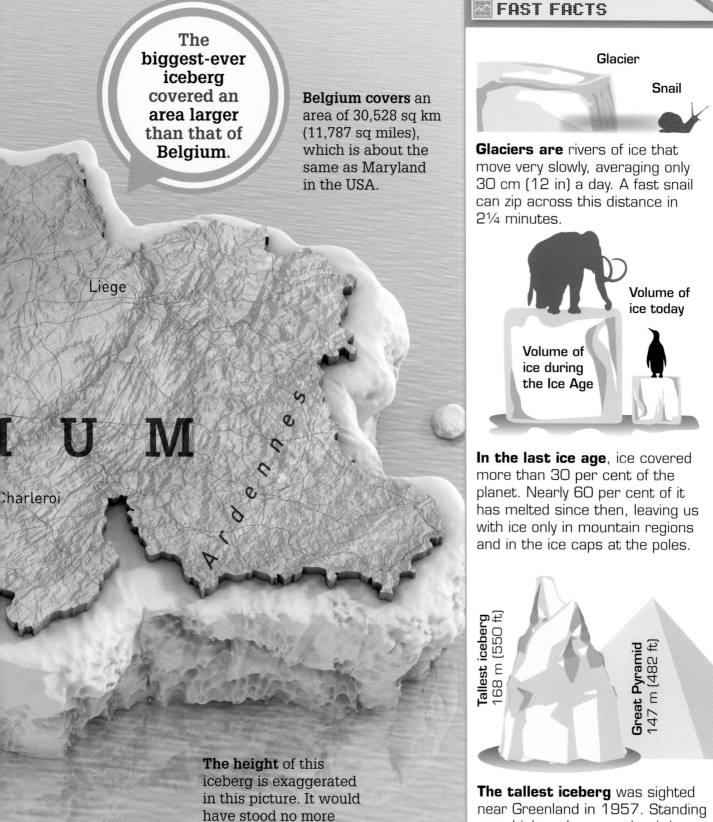

The **biggest-ever iceberg** covered an area larger than that of **Belgium**.

Belgium covers an area of 30,528 sq km (11,787 sq miles), which is about the same as Maryland in the USA.

Liege

I U M

Charleroi

Ardennes

The height of this iceberg is exaggerated in this picture. It would have stood no more than 150 m (500 ft) above the sea surface.

FAST FACTS

Glacier

Snail

Glaciers are rivers of ice that move very slowly, averaging only 30 cm (12 in) a day. A fast snail can zip across this distance in 2¼ minutes.

Volume of ice today

Volume of ice during the Ice Age

In the last ice age, ice covered more than 30 per cent of the planet. Nearly 60 per cent of it has melted since then, leaving us with ice only in mountain regions and in the ice caps at the poles.

Tallest iceberg 168 m (550 ft)

Great Pyramid 147 m (482 ft)

The tallest iceberg was sighted near Greenland in 1957. Standing even higher above sea level than the Great Pyramid, the iceberg may have extended a further 1,500 m (4,900 ft) below the surface.

What if **all** the ice melted?

Ten per cent of the **world's land** is covered by thick **glaciers** and **ice sheets**. If it all melted, the **sea level** would rise by up to **70 m** (230 ft). Many **major world cities** would be **covered** by the **ocean.**

SHRINKING GLACIERS

Glaciers are great rivers of slowly flowing ice. The ice builds up over many years from fallen snow. Glaciers can begin on any high ground where the snow does not thaw completely in spring. In parts of the Arctic, glaciers reach down to the sea, but most are shrinking. Between 1941 and 2004, the Muir Glacier in Alaska (above) retreated more than 12 km (7 miles) and the sea filled its valley.

Low-lying cities by the coast would be devastated by big sea level rises. Manhattan, New York, would be almost completely swallowed by the ocean, along with the bases of its famous landmarks.

The first 18 floors of the Empire State Building would be flooded if the sea level rose by 70 m (230 ft).

If the world's ice melted, the Statue of Liberty would stand waist-deep in water.

The base of the statue's pedestal is only about 6 m (20 ft) above current sea level.

FAST FACTS

Current coastline

Coastline after flooding

If all the ice melted, the coastlines of many countries would dramatically change. Britain and Ireland would turn into a group of smaller islands. Low-lying countries such as Bangladesh and the Netherlands would almost disappear.

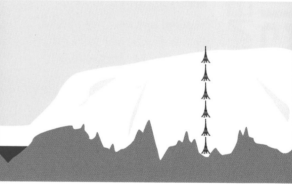

The ice over Antarctica is extremely thick, averaging 1,830 m (6,000 ft) – nearly as deep as six Eiffel Towers. In some places it is more than twice as deep, at 4,776 m (15,670 ft).

The Statue of Liberty's pedestal is 47 m (154 ft) high.

Where is the snowiest place on Earth?

The **greatest snowfall** over one year was **29.86 m** (95 ft) in **Mount Baker Ski Area,** Washington, USA, measured in the **1998–1999** season.

Mount Baker's record snowfall **would bury over half the** Leaning Tower of Pisa.

EXTREME SNOW

Japan's sightseeing road, the Tateyama Kurobe Alpine Route, is closed all winter. It opens in spring, when diggers cut through 20 m (66 ft) of snow to the road below.

The Leaning Tower of Pisa is 55.9 m (183.3 ft) from the ground on its higher side.

This 30-m (100-ft) pile of snow is much less dense than water. To compare it to a rainfall total, experts would melt it down in a snow gauge, which would give just 2.5 m (8 ft) of water.

The most snowfall in one month was in Tamarac, California, USA, where 11.4 m (37 ft 5 in) of snow fell in March 1911.

New York City receives an average of 68 cm (2ft 5 in inches) of snow every year.

FAST FACTS

Compared to snowfall records, extremes of rainfall are far higher, in terms of total amount of water.

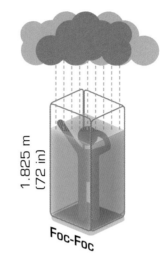

1.825 m (72 in)

Foc-Foc

The highest ever rainfall in 24 hours took place in January 1966 in Foc-Foc, on the island of Réunion, where 1.825 m (6 ft) of rain fell.

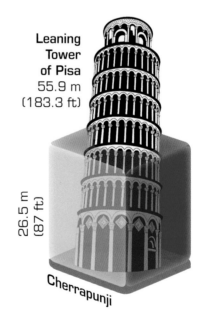

Leaning Tower of Pisa 55.9 m (183.3 ft)

26.5 m (87 ft)

Cherrapunji

Cherrapunji, India, saw the most rainfall in one year in 1860–1861, when 26.5 m (87 ft) of rain fell — enough to flood almost half the Leaning Tower of Pisa.

How big was the largest hailstone?

The **largest hailstone** ever known fell in **Vivian, South Dakota**, USA, in a storm on **23 July 2010**. It was **20 cm (8 in)** across.

DIVIDED IN TWO

This hailstone cut in half shows the layers of ice that form hail. Hailstones grow because winds in storm clouds throw them upwards again and again. Each time, water freezes on to them, building up another layer of ice.

Giant hailstones like this form in clouds with very powerful updrafts, such as those in intense thunderstorms and tornadoes. When giant hail is finally heavy enough to fall to the ground, it can dent cars, smash windshields, flatten crops, and injure living things.

The **South Dakota** hailstone was about **three times** the **width** of a tennis ball.

FAST FACTS

Hail most often forms in giant thunderclouds, which are also the source of lightning.

Cloud top
12,000 m (40,000 ft)

Mount Everest
8,848 m (29,029 ft)

Cloud base
2,000 m (6,600 ft)

Thunderclouds, technically known as cumulonimbus, are the tallest kind of clouds. They are sometimes more than 12,000 m (40,000 ft) high – half again as high as the highest mountain. They are column-shaped with a wide, flat top.

A bolt of lightning can have a temperature of around 30,000°C (54,000°F) – more than five times hotter than the surface of the Sun, which is the hottest object in our Solar System by several thousand degrees.

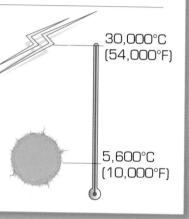

30,000°C (54,000°F)

5,600°C (10,000°F)

The lumps that covered the hailstone are the result of smaller hailstones colliding with each other and sticking together. Each lump is a former smaller hailstone with layers of ice added on top.

Record hailstone
20 cm (8 in) across,
1 kg (2.2 lb) in weight

Tennis ball
6.7 cm (2.6 in)
across

Weather data

HOT

The **hottest** temperature ever recorded at ground level in the shade was in **Death Valley, California**, in 1913 – a scorching

56.6°C
(134°F).

AND COLD

The **coldest** temperature ever recorded at ground level was at **Vostok, Antarctica**, in 1983. It was a bone-chilling

–89.2°C (–129°F).

CLOUD COVER

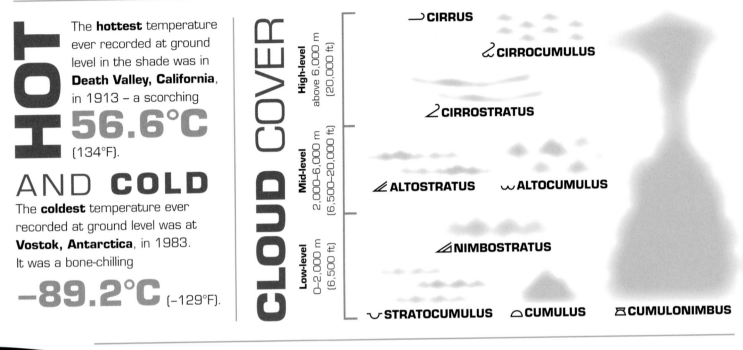

High-level above 6,000 m (20,000 ft)

⌐ **CIRRUS**

⌐ **CIRROCUMULUS**

⌐ **CIRROSTRATUS**

Mid-level 2,000–6,000 m (6,500–20,000 ft)

⌐ **ALTOSTRATUS**   ⌐ **ALTOCUMULUS**

Low-level 0–2,000 m (6,500 ft)

⌐ **NIMBOSTRATUS**

⌐ **STRATOCUMULUS**   ⌐ **CUMULUS**   ⌐ **CUMULONIMBUS**

THE ATMOSPHERE

Surrounding the planet is a **layer of gases** called the **atmosphere**. Earth's atmosphere contains five separate layers.

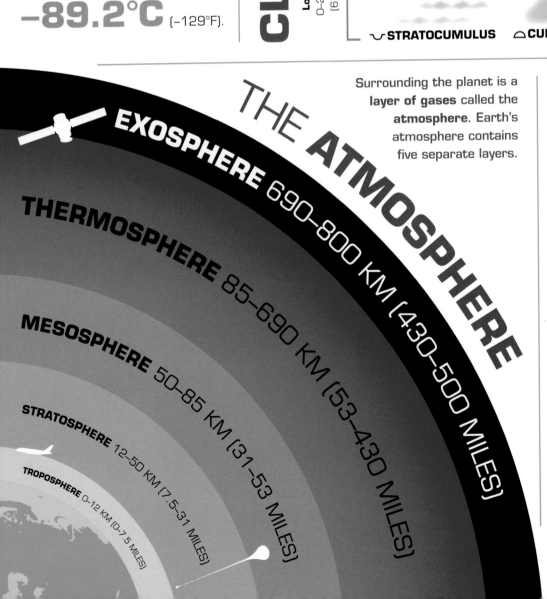

EXOSPHERE 690–800 KM (430–500 MILES)

THERMOSPHERE 85–690 KM (53–430 MILES)

MESOSPHERE 50–85 KM (31–53 MILES)

STRATOSPHERE 12–50 KM (7.5–31 MILES)

TROPOSPHERE 0–12 KM (0–7.5 MILES)

RAINY DAYS

The **wettest** place on Earth is Mawsynram in northeast India, with average annual rainfall of

11,870 mm
(467 in) per year.

The place with the **most rainy days** each year is Mt Waialeale, Kauai, Hawaii, with **350** rainy days a year. On average it is dry just **one day** a month.

The longest continuous rainfall lasted **247 days**, from 27 August 1993 to 30 April 1994, in Kaneohe Ranch, Oahu, Hawaii.

WINDY DAYS

The Beaufort scale lists the effects of increasing wind speeds.

BEAUFORT NUMBER	WIND SPEED	WIND EFFECT ON LAND
0	0	Smoke rises vertically
1	1–3 kph (1–2 mph)	Smoke drifts gently
2	4–11 kph (3–7 mph)	Leaves rustle
3	12–19 kph (8–12 mph)	Twigs move
4	20–29 kph (13–18 mph)	Small branches move
5	30–39 kph (19–24 mph)	Small trees sway
6	40–50 kph (25–31 mph)	Umbrellas hard to use
7	51–61 kph (32–38 mph)	Whole trees sway
8	62–74 kph (39–46 mph)	Difficulty walking
9	75–87 kph (47–54 mph)	Roofs damaged
10	88–101 kph (55–63 mph)	Trees blown down
11	102–119 kph (64–74 mph	Houses damaged
12	over 119 kph (over 74 mph)	Buildings destroyed

TWISTERS
500

At ground level, **tornadoes** have the *fastest winds.* The most powerful recorded had wind speeds of kph (300 mph) or more. Tornadoes can also move at speeds of up to **110 kph** (70 mph) – far too fast for anyone to outrun.

HURRICANE DAMAGE

Hurricanes are categorized according to their speed and destructiveness using the Saffir-Simpson scale.

CATEGORY	WIND SPEED	EFFECTS	
CATEGORY **1**	**120–153 kph** (74–95 mph)	Minor building damage; branches snapped	
CATEGORY **2**	**154–177 kph** (96–110 mph)	Some roof, door, and window damage	
CATEGORY **3**	**178–208 kph** (111–130 mph)	Roof tiles dislodged; large trees uprooted	
CATEGORY **4**	**209–251 kph** (131–155 mph)	Roofs blown off; major coastal flooding	
CATEGORY **5**	**over 252 kph** (over 155 mph)	Buildings destroyed; catastrophic flooding	

BOLTS FROM THE BLUE

Lightning strikes somewhere on Earth **100** times a second. It strikes the Empire State Building roughly **100** times a year.

What was the biggest natural disaster ?

The **disease** known as the **Black Death**, which swept the world in the 14th century, **killed** up to **75 million people**.

The Rose Bowl sports stadium, Pasadena, California, USA, has an official capacity of about 91,000 people.

SPANISH FLU

In 1918, after World War I, there was a global outbreak of the disease "Spanish Flu". Spread by the mass movement of troops, it killed over 50 million people – more than the war itself. Diseases on a global scale are called pandemics.

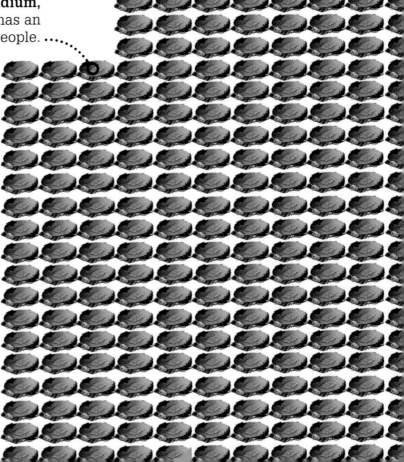

The Black Death, or plague, was caused by bacteria carried by fleas on rats. It began in Asia but spread quickly as rats boarded merchant ships, taking the disease with them. The plague reached Europe in 1346, where it killed at least 30 per cent of the people.

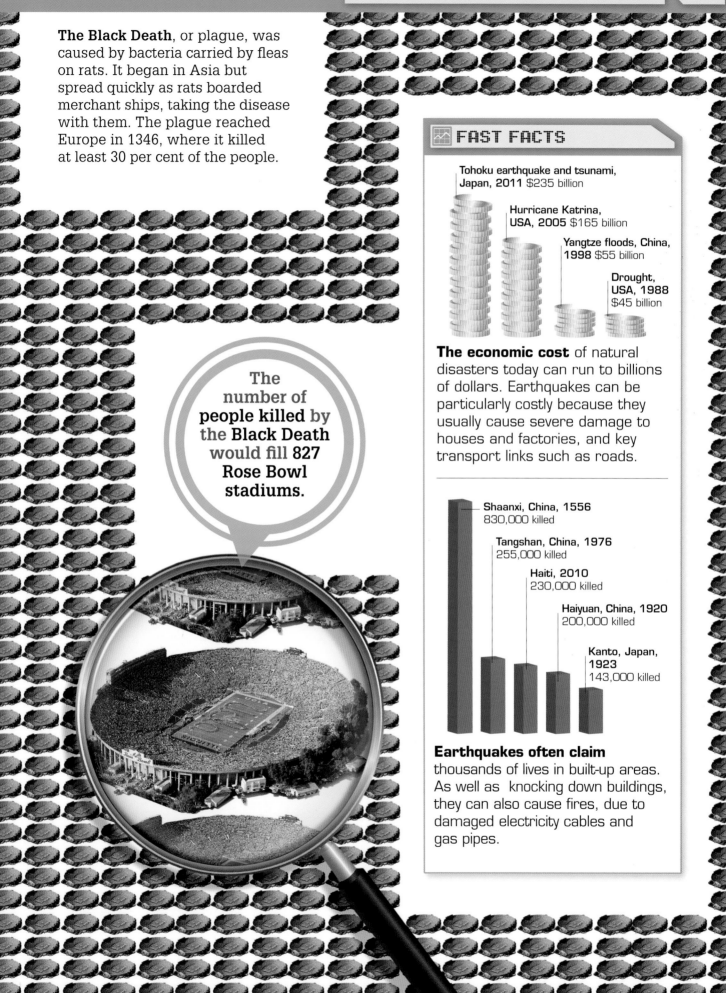

The number of **people killed by the Black Death** would fill **827 Rose Bowl stadiums.**

FAST FACTS

Tohoku earthquake and tsunami, Japan, 2011 $235 billion

Hurricane Katrina, USA, 2005 $165 billion

Yangtze floods, China, 1998 $55 billion

Drought, USA, 1988 $45 billion

The economic cost of natural disasters today can run to billions of dollars. Earthquakes can be particularly costly because they usually cause severe damage to houses and factories, and key transport links such as roads.

Shaanxi, China, 1556 830,000 killed

Tangshan, China, 1976 255,000 killed

Haiti, 2010 230,000 killed

Haiyuan, China, 1920 200,000 killed

Kanto, Japan, 1923 143,000 killed

Earthquakes often claim thousands of lives in built-up areas. As well as knocking down buildings, they can also cause fires, due to damaged electricity cables and gas pipes.

How **many people** are there in **China?**

The **population** of **China**, including Taiwan, is about **1.4 billion**. In around 2022, **India** is likely to displace China as the world's most populous country.

Australia is the world's sixth-largest country, after Russia, Canada, China, the USA, and Brazil.

Australi

China

CHINESE COMMUNITIES

One in every five people on Earth is Chinese. Most major cities outside of China have large Chinese communities, making Chinese culture an important influence actoss the world.

There are as many people in China today as there were in the whole world around 150 years ago!

The area of China is only slightly greater than that of the USA, and Australia is not far behind. But China's population is more than four times bigger than the USA's and nearly 60 times larger than that of Australia. Here, the three countries are shown in proportion to their populations.

China has a population almost 60 times larger than that of Australia.

United States

The USA has about 323 million people – 23 times more than live in Australia.

FAST FACTS

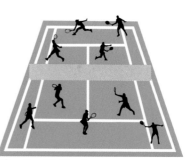

Australia
Population of about 24 million
Density of 3 people per sq km

Sri Lanka
Population of about 21 million
Density of 320 people per sq km

Australia and Sri Lanka have roughly similar-sized populations, but Australia is about 120 times larger. If Australia were as densely populated as Sri Lanka, it would be home to nearly 2.5 billion people!

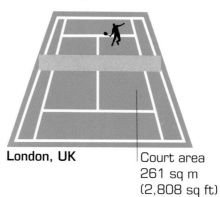

Manila, Philippines

London, UK | Court area 261 sq m (2,808 sq ft)

Some cities are more crowded than others. If Manila and London were divided into tennis courts, Manila would have nine people on each court and London only one.

How **fast** is the **population** of the world **growing**?

Around **360,000 babies** are **born each day** and about **160,000 people die**. So overall, the world's population **grows by 200,000 people** every **day** of the year.

AGEING WORLD

The world's population is getting older. Better health care means that more babies are surviving, and so people are having fewer children. It also enables older people to live longer.

At least another two people would be added to the crowd every second.

FAST FACTS

The human population is growing faster in some places than in others. Using a graph called a population pyramid, we can see which countries have fast-growing populations.

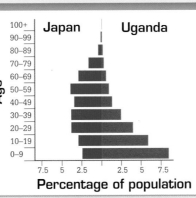

Age

100+
90–99
80–89
70–79
60–69
50–59
40–49
30–39
20–29
10–19
0–9

Japan   Uganda

7.5   5   2.5   2.5   5   7.5

Percentage of population

Japan's narrow-based, bulging pyramid shows an older population with relatively few young people. The birth rate is low and the population is falling.

Uganda's sloping pyramid shows the country has a high birth rate, many children, few older people, and a fast-growing population.

This crowd of **8,000 people** shows how much **Earth's population** increases **every** single hour.

In just one hour, the world's population grows by more than 8,000 people. That's the same as 23 plane-loads of passengers arriving on the planet every 60 minutes. Over one day, there would be enough new inhabitants of Earth to fill London's Olympic Stadium 2.5 times.

Humans and other life forms

Earth is rich in wonderful life forms – including us! Our bodies perform fantastic feats each day just to keep us alive. We share our world with a host of other incredible plants and animals – some massive, others tiny – many of which have extraordinary abilities.

The manta ray is a gentle giant that "flies" through the water by beating its huge wing-like fins. Mantas can grow up to 7 m (23 ft) wide – the same as the average height of 3.5 men. They can weigh up to 1,350 kg (3,000 lb) – the same as two adult cows.

How much blood does a heart pump?

Oxygen-poor **blood** returns to the heart through veins (shown in blue).

The average **adult human heart** pumps about **5 litres** (10.6 pints) of blood **every minute**, which is the **total amount** of blood in a **man's body**.

EXTREME PHYSIQUES

When cyclist Miguel Indurain won five Tours de France in the 1990s, his heart could pump 50 litres (106 pints) of blood a minute and his lungs could hold 8 litres (16.9 pints) of oxygen. Average adult lungs hold less than 6 litres (12.7 pints).

The muscle that makes up the wall of the heart has its own blood supply.

FAST FACTS

The amount of blood pumped by the heart in a minute is known as "cardiac output". This can be used to measure a person's level of fitness. The more blood pumped, the more work their bodies can do.

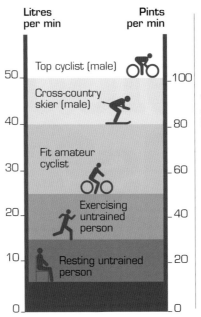

Litres per min		Pints per min
50	Top cyclist (male)	100
40	Cross-country skier (male)	80
30	Fit amateur cyclist	60
20	Exercising untrained person	40
10	Resting untrained person	20
0		0

Women
4.5 litres
(9.5 pints)

Men
5 litres
(10.6 pints)

Pregnant women
6.5 litres
(13.7 pints)

On average, women have slightly less blood than men. An average pregnant woman, however, has more blood than a man. This extra blood is used to carry nutrients and oxygen to her baby.

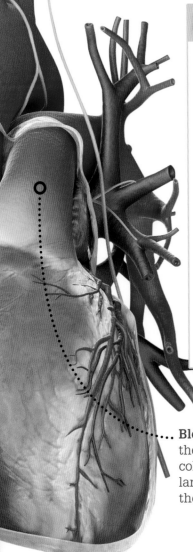

Blood travels from the heart to the lungs to collect oxygen through a large blood vessel called the pulmonary artery.

An adult heart pumps enough blood to fill 5.3 38,000-litre (10,000-gallon) road tankers every month.

The heart has a left and a right side. The right side delivers blood to the lungs to pick up oxygen. The left side pumps this oxygen-rich blood around the body to deliver nutrients to all the body's cells. The cells absorb the oxygen, and the oxygen-poor blood returns to the heart to start its journey again.

The heart pumps oxygen-rich blood to the body through arteries (shown in red). This blood is bright red because it contains haemoglobin, the substance that carries the oxygen. Oxygen-poor blood is dark red.

How much air do you breathe in a lifetime?

Based on a lifespan of 70 years, the average human breathes around 275 million litres (9.7 million cubic feet) of air.

An average-sized hot-air balloon, capable of carrying three to five people, contains 2,800,000 litres (616,000 gallons) of air.

Over a lifetime, the average human breathes enough air to fill around 95–100 hot-air balloons.

FLAT-HEADED FROG

Most frogs breathe through both their lungs and skin, but this rare Bornean flat-headed frog, which grows up to 7.7 cm (3 in) long, has no lungs. It is the only known frog to breathe entirely through its skin.

The windpipe is the tube in the chest and throat that carries air in and out of the lungs.

Human lungs

An adult's lungs take in an average of about 0.5 litres (1 pint) of air in each breath, and breathe about 15 times a minute, when sitting down.

FAST FACTS

Lungs

Alveoli

Tennis court

The average adult's lungs
contain 300–500 million tiny round sacs called alveoli – enough to cover about half a tennis court.

Bar-headed goose
6,300 m (21,670 ft)

Himalayan mountain pass
5,500 m
(18,000 ft)

Bar-headed geese have very efficient lungs and can cross the Himalayas at altitudes of around 6,300 m (21,670 ft), where there is very little oxygen. Humans cannot live permanently at such extreme heights.

Large eyes give animals the brightest, sharpest vision possible. Tarsiers own some of the largest eyes relative to their body size. They need them to hunt for insects in the rainforest at night. Each of their eyes is as big as their brain! A human's eyes are proportionally much smaller.

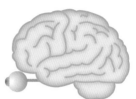

Tarsier brain and eye relative sizes

Human brain and eye relative sizes

What has the biggest eyes?

The **colossal squid**, a little-known species of squid bigger than the giant squid, has **eyes** up to **27 cm** (11 in) across in the few individuals measured.

PREHISTORIC VISION

Extinct reptiles called ichthyosaurs had eyes up to 30 cm (12 in) across. Like huge squid species, some probably hunted in the deep sea, their big eyes helping them to see in the dim light.

Human eyeball (life size) 2.4 cm (1 in) across

Horse eyeball (life size) 4 cm (2 in) across

The lens of the colossal squid's eye is ball-shaped and about the size of an orange. ....

The largest **colossal squid eye** ever studied was a dead one that had the **same diameter as 11 human eyeballs**.

Blue whale eyeball (life size) 15 cm (6 in) across

Colossal squid eyeball (life size) 27 cm (11 in) across. (Experts think the colossal squid's eyes may grow to 30–40 cm (12–16 in) across – as big as a beachball!)

What is the biggest animal?

The **largest animal** on the **planet** is the **blue whale** measuring **30 m** (100 ft). It is the **biggest** animal that has **ever lived**, including **dinosaurs**.

Tail flukes up to 7.6 m (25 ft) across can power the blue whale at speeds of 50 kph (31 mph).

FAST FACTS

Blue whale

School buses

A blue whale is longer than a basketball court and weighs up to 180 tonnes (200 tons) – the same as 15 school buses.

Blue whales make a noise louder than a jet aircraft taking off. Whales produce very low frequency sounds at a level of 188 decibels that can be heard from thousands of miles away.

188 dB

140 dB

FILTER FEEDING

A blue whale can eat around 3.5 tonnes (4 tons) of tiny sea creatures, called krill, a day. Taking 90-tonne (99-ton) gulps of water, the whale then filters the water out through baleen plates – comb-like structures that hang from its jaw, trapping the krill.

The blue whale's heart is the size of a small car.

Its eyeball is 15 cm (6 in) in diameter.

Its tongue weighs as much as an elephant.

Its outer ear is the width of a pencil tip.

A blue whale is as long as 17 scuba divers swimming in a line.

A blue whale can blow 4,500 litres (160 cu ft) of air out of its blowholes at 480 kph (300 mph). The spray it produces reaches a height of 9 m (30 ft) – as tall as five men standing on each others' head.

What was the biggest dinosaur?

The **fossil bones** of the **largest animal ever to walk on land** were unearthed in 2015. It is a type of **titanosaur** that **fossil hunters** estimate weighed **77 tonnes** (85 tons) and measured **37 m** (122 ft) long.

The dinosaur's tail may have been used for support as it reared up on its hind legs to reach tree branches.

The titanosaur was as long as four buses and weighed as much as 14 African elephants.

FAST FACTS

The new titanosaur is the biggest of a family called the sauropods. Even one of the smallest, *Europasaurus*, was 6 m (20 ft) long and weighed up to 1 tonne (1.1 tons).

Europasaurus   Titanosaur

Human

Pliosaur

Among the biggest prehistoric beasts living in the sea were pliosaurs. The largest of these were over 15 m (50 ft) long.

BEFORE THE DINOSAURS

Long before the dinosaurs, there were no large animals on land — but there were in the oceans. *Pterygotus*, a giant sea scorpion that lived 400 million years ago, grew to 2.3 m (7.5 ft) long — bigger than an adult human.

The 84 fossil bones were discovered in Argentina in 2015 and the species has not yet been named. The bones revealed that it was a teenager and was still growing!

The small head did not contain heavy jaws for chewing food – titanosaurs simply gulped it down.

Its long neck meant that the titanosaur could eat from the ground or from trees. It had to eat a lot – a skip full of vegetation every day.

154
utton Green
gton W.Croydon
wood Junction

LONDON   RT

A 110

RT.3775

LONDON TRANSPORT

New titanosaur
37 m (122 ft) long

Double-decker bus
9.5 m (31.2 ft) long

What was the biggest land predator?

The **biggest predator** that ever lived **on land** was *Spinosaurus*, a **17-m- (56-ft-)** long fish-eating **dinosaur**.

Spinosaurus was the longest predatory dinosaur known. It lived around 100 million years ago in North Africa.

This adult man stands at about 1.8 m (5.11 ft) tall.

A male polar bear is the biggest land predator today. It can grow up to to 3 m (10 ft) in length and 1.5 m (5 ft) tall at the shoulder.

Spinosaurus's **size** was enhanced by long spines extending up from its backbone, which probably created a tall crest or "sail".

Spinosaurus was more than five times the length of a polar bear.

SABRE-TOOTHED CAT

Smilodon was the biggest cat that ever lived. At 2 m (6.5 ft) long, it was big enough to attack and eat mammoths. The cat probably wrestled its prey to the ground, then killed it with its large canine teeth.

The dinosaur's huge tail balanced the weight of its head and forelimbs, allowing it to walk on its hind legs.

📈 FAST FACTS

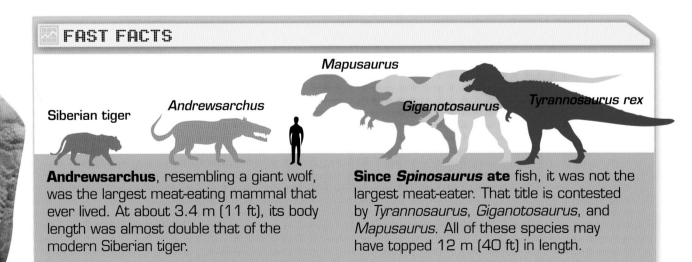

Siberian tiger

Andrewsarchus

Mapusaurus

Giganotosaurus

Tyrannosaurus rex

Andrewsarchus, resembling a giant wolf, was the largest meat-eating mammal that ever lived. At about 3.4 m (11 ft), its body length was almost double that of the modern Siberian tiger.

Since *Spinosaurus* ate fish, it was not the largest meat-eater. That title is contested by *Tyrannosaurus*, *Giganotosaurus*, and *Mapusaurus*. All of these species may have topped 12 m (40 ft) in length.

What was the biggest snake?

Titanoboa was an **enormous snake** measuring **14.6 m** (48 ft), or longer than a school bus. It lived around **60 million years ago** in the **jungle swamps** of modern-day **Colombia**.

EATING HABITS

Big snakes such as pythons can eat prey wider than themselves. The snake cannot chew, so prey must be swallowed whole. Digesting food uses so much energy, the snake is inactive for several days.

Like the jaws of today's snakes, the lower jaw would unhinge, enabling *Titanoboa* to swallow large prey.

Snakes breathe through a hole called the glottis. This can move to the side so that the reptile can breathe as it slowly swallows its prey.

Titanoboa's colouring is unknown. The pattern on this illustration is based on the anaconda, one of the biggest snakes alive today.

The middle of the trunk was much wider than the ends of the snake. At its widest, it was 90 cm (3 ft) in diameter.

The **thickest** part of *Titanoboa*'s body was **half the height of a man**.

Titanoboa **weighed** more than 1 tonne (1 ton) – as much as a small family car and big enough to tackle giant turtles and crocodiles. Experts have argued that it grew so big because the world was warmer 60 million years ago, and reptiles today are usually bigger in warmer climates.

📈 **FAST FACTS**

The longest snakes alive today are little more than half the length of *Titanoboa*.

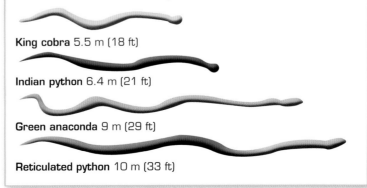

King cobra 5.5 m (18 ft)

Indian python 6.4 m (21 ft)

Green anaconda 9 m (29 ft)

Reticulated python 10 m (33 ft)

Megalodon's tail fin provided all the propulsion the shark needed while swimming and hunting.

How **big** was the **biggest** shark?

MOSASAUR

Megalodon was one of the world's biggest-ever hunters, but many other ocean predators have grown to monstrous lengths. The 15-m (49-ft) *Mosasaurus* lived around 65 million years ago.

The **largest shark** that ever lived was **megalodon**, which may have grown to **20 m** (66 ft) **long.** It died out more than **1.5 million years ago.**

Megalodon's dorsal **fin** may have been taller than a man.

Megalodon may have grown to be between 7 and 11 times the length of an adult scuba diver.

Some experts think megalodon was very similar to today's great white shark, but much bigger. It may not have been closely related, however. It lived in all the world's oceans and first appeared around 17–16 million years ago.

The pectoral fin provided lift, stopping the shark from sinking.

FAST FACTS

Today's biggest shark is not the great white, but the whale shark, a gentle giant that feeds on plankton – tiny floating creatures. The great white is the biggest predatory shark – one that hunts down individual prey, such as fish.

Megalodon
16–20 m
(52–65 ft) long,
50 tonnes (55 tons)

Whale shark
12.65 m (41.5 ft)
long, 21.5 tonnes
(23.5 tons)

Great white shark
6.1 m (20 ft) long,
1.9 tonnes (2 tons)

Megalodon's huge teeth are the most common fossil remains of the creature. They are the same shape as the teeth of the great white shark, but more than three times the height.

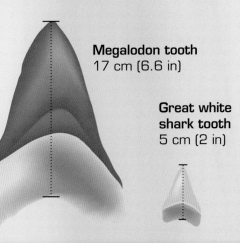

Megalodon tooth
17 cm (6.6 in)

Great white shark tooth
5 cm (2 in)

The spider's leg span is measured from the tip of one leg to the tip of the opposite leg.

The spider's fangs, which are 2.5 cm (1 in) long, are tucked under the hair-covered upper mouthparts.

The Goliath bird-eater is a species of tarantula and lives in South America. It grows big enough to eat birds, although it mostly eats insects, rodents, bats, snakes, and lizards. It pounces on prey and injects it with venom from its fangs.

The hairs covering the spider's body can cause rashes and swelling on human skin. The tarantula flicks them at attackers to defend itself.

GIANT HUNTSMAN SPIDER

The longest spider legs are thought to belong to the giant huntsman spider of Laos, southeast Asia. Its legs span up to 30 cm (12 in), although its body is just 4.6 cm (1.8 in) long.

Goliaths can grow to be **bigger** than an **adult's hand** and can cover a **dinner plate!**

How **big** can spiders grow?

The Goliath bird-eater rubs bristles on its legs to produce a hissing sound as a warning to predators.

The **heaviest type** of spider is the **goliath bird-eating spider**, which can **weigh** up to **175 g** (6 oz). The biggest measured had a **leg span** of **28 cm** (11 in).

📊 FAST FACTS

Darwin's bark spiders can spin webs as wide as a six-lane motorway (25 m, 80 ft). Its silk is highly resistant to breaking and more than 10 times tougher than Kevlar (a material used to make body armour).

All spiders are venomous, and some species have venom that is deadly enough to kill dozens of mice. Most spiders are harmless to humans, but these three demand respect.

Mice killed by 1 millionth of a gram of venom

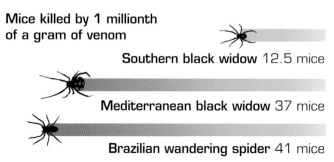

Southern black widow 12.5 mice

Mediterranean black widow 37 mice

Brazilian wandering spider 41 mice

What is the biggest insect?

There are several contenders, but the **Atlas moth** has the biggest wings, with a **span** of **25 cm** (10 in) and a **wing area** of **400 sq cm** (62 sq in).

The Atlas moth is much **bigger** than an adult **human hand**.

GIANT WETA

The giant weta, one of the world's heaviest insects, lives in New Zealand. Wetas gnaw roots and stems in their forest habitat and have grown to mouse-like sizes. At 70 g (2.5 oz), the largest are as big as three house mice.

The fat abdomen of the female contains an egg factory.

The Atlas moth of Southeast Asia is the biggest insect by wing area. However, the white witch moth of Central and South America has the widest wingspan, at about 31 cm (12 in).

These narrow antennae tell us this is a female, which is even larger and heavier than a male. The male has bigger, more feathery antennae, and he uses them to detect pheromones (scent) released by females.

The wing tip looks like a snake's head, which possibly frightens would-be predators.

The triangular patterns on the moth's wings are thought to help camouflage.

FAST FACTS

There are other insects competing for the title of the biggest insect alive. Here are some of the contenders.

The titan beetle of South American rainforests grows up to 16.5 cm (6.5 in) long – as long as the body of a rat. Its jaws can snap a pencil in half.

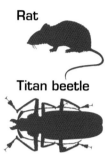

Rat

Titan beetle

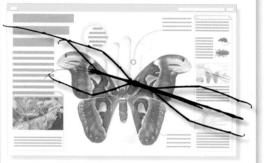

Stick insects can be even longer. The record-breaking Chan's megastick of Borneo, Malaysia, is 56.7 cm (22.3 in) long with outstretched legs. That's longer than this book.

Goliath beetle grub

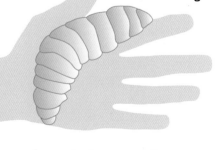

Some insects have really large grubs. One of the biggest and heaviest is that of Africa's Goliath beetle. It can grow up to 13 cm (5 in) long and weighs 100 g (3.5 oz).

Running along the front edge of *Quetzalcoatlus*'s wing were the incredibly long bones of a single finger, which held the wing open.

The wings of *Quetzalcoatlus* stretched further than those of a Tiger Moth biplane.

What had the longest wings ever?

The **largest flying creature** was a **pterosaur** called *Quetzalcoatlus*. It soared over its relatives, the **dinosaurs**, 68 million years ago. The largest had a **wingspan** of **more than 10 m** (33 ft).

FAST FACTS

Here's how *Quetzalcoatlus*'s wingspan compares to some other giant flyers.

Argentavis lived 6 million years ago and at 7 m (23 ft) across the wings was the largest flying bird ever.

The great bustard is today's heaviest flying bird and has a wingspan of 2.5 m (8.2 ft).

Quetzalcoatlus lived 68–66 million years ago and measured 10 m (33 ft) from wingtip to wingtip.

The wandering albatross has the longest wings of any living bird, at 3.5 m (11.5 ft).

Quetzalcoatlus was very thin and light in the central body and neck, so despite its colossal dimensions, even this 10-m (33-ft) individual probably weighed less than 250 kg (550 lb). This is still twice as heavy as an ostrich.

A Tiger Moth has a wingspan of 8.9 m (29 ft). Originally designed to train military pilots in the 1930s, it can carry two people. It is still famous and popular with pilots today.

MONSTER BIRDS

Teratornis (left) was an ancient bird that was similar to a modern condor, but bigger and heavier. Its close relative, *Argentavis*, was gigantic and weighed as much as a person.

At only 5.5 cm (2.2 in) long, the **bee hummingbird** can **perch on the end of a pencil.**

The male bee hummingbird has a glossy pink head and throat and is even smaller than the female.

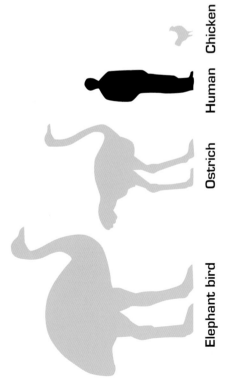

FAST FACTS

Actual size

The bee hummingbird builds a cup-shaped nest about 2.5 cm (1 in) across from bits of cobwebs, bark, and lichen. Nests have been built on single clothes pegs. The eggs are no bigger than peas.

In contrast, the heaviest living bird that can fly is the great bustard. At 20.9 kg (46 lb), it weighs as much as a six-year-old boy.

Great bustard

Elephant bird   Ostrich   Human   Chicken

Today's heaviest bird, the ostrich, can weigh nearly twice as much as an adult person. However, a few hundred years ago, an even heavier bird – the elephant bird – lived in Madagascar. It weighed as much as three ostriches. It is now extinct.

The bee hummingbird is a tiny but busy bird. It hovers by flapping its wings at 80 times a second, with its heart beating at an incredible 1,220 times a minute. To power this activity, the bird must feed every 10–15 minutes. It eats about half its own body weight in sugary nectar every day.

What is the smallest bird?

The **bee hummingbird**, which lives only in Cuba, is 5.5 cm (2.2 in) **long** and **weighs** just 1.6 g (0.06 oz).

SWORD-BILLED HUMMINGBIRD

Not all hummingbirds are tiny. Among the largest are sword-billed hummingbirds. Their bill alone measures the same as two entire bee hummingbirds!

Which bird laid the biggest egg?

Eggs of the extinct **elephant bird** were up to **34 cm** (13 in) **long.** Elephant birds lived in **Madagascar** until a few hundred years ago.

Emu

Emu eggs are unusually dark. They look like a huge avocado, at 13 cm (5 in) high.

A kiwi is 20 times smaller than an emu, but its eggs are almost the same size.

Hummingbird eggs are the smallest bird eggs. This one is from a ruby-throated hummingbird.

Rusty tinamou

Chicken

Hummingbird

King penguin

Quail

Kiwi

Common sandpiper

Cormorant

Tawny owl

The most familia eggs are laid by the domestic chicken.

FAST FACTS

Elephant bird eggs are bigger than those of most dinosaurs. Even the eggs of sauropods (the biggest dinosaurs) are no more than 20 cm (8 in) long. Recent digs in China, however, appear to have turned up giant eggs of two-legged dinosaurs similar to *Oviraptor*.

33 cm (13 in)

20 cm (8 in)

60 cm (24 in)

Elephant bird 3 m (10 ft) tall

Sauropod up to 36 m (120 ft) long

Giant *Oviraptor* 8 m (26 ft) long

Elephant birds had died out by the 18th century, but a few of their eggshells still exist. Most shell remains, however, are found as fragments. Pieces found near the sites of ancient cooking fires suggest that people ate the eggs.

In terms of volume, an **elephant bird's egg** is as big as **200 chicken eggs** or 11 ostrich eggs.

The shell of the egg is 3.8 mm (0.15 in) thick and could bear the weight of about 90 bricks (248 kg, 550 lb).

Ostrich

The ostrich is the world's largest bird, and it lays the biggest eggs today – although they are the smallest in relation to the size of the mother. They weigh on average 1.4 kg (3.1 lbs) – more than 20 chicken's eggs.

Elephant bird

Cetti's warbler

Guillemot

KIWI EGGS

Kiwis lay the biggest eggs in relation to their body size. One egg can be up to one-fifth of the weight of its mother.

Guillemot eggs roll in circles, so they don't fall off cliff ledges, where they are laid.

Great auk

Carrion crow

Curlew

Sparrowhawk

Cuckoo

Redshank

How far can a bird fly?

Bar-tailed godwits have been tracked flying **11,680 km** (7,258 miles) **non-stop** from Alaska to New Zealand on their **yearly migration.**

North Korea

South Korea

China

Japan

Philippines

Indonesia

Papua New Guinea

Australia

FAST FACTS

Earth

Moon

Arctic terns migrate from the Arctic to the Antarctic and back every year. Single birds have been tracked flying 70,900 km (44,000 miles) in this time. In their 30-year lifetime, they can cover 2.1 million km (1.3 million miles), or more than two round-trips to the Moon.

Glider 3,009 km (1,870 miles)

Airliner (Boeing 777 specially adapted for record attempt), 21,602 km (13,423 miles)

Breitling Orbiter balloon 40,814 km (25,361 miles)

Virgin Atlantic GlobalFlyer 41,467 km (25,766 miles)

An airliner can fly farther than any bird if it is specially adapted. Above are four human non-stop flight records involving different kinds of aircraft.

Every year in March, Pacific bar-tailed godwits fly north from New Zealand. They arrive in Alaska to nest in May, after refuelling in China. Scientists know the return journey to New Zealand can be direct and non-stop.

Russia

Alaska

Breeding grounds in the Yukon Delta of Alaska become a godwit's home in the summer, when the bird brings up its chicks.

A **bar-tailed godwit** can, without landing, **fly farther than most airliners.**

The Airbus 320 is a short-to-medium-range ner. Flying from Alaska, ould run out of fuel long before the godwit, and ld have to land at Wake Island in the Pacific.

The godwit's curved route goes over Hawaii, extending the journey.

5,676 km (3,527 miles)

Pacific Ocean

10,595 km (6,583 miles)

11,686 km (7,261 miles)

The Boeing 777-300 is long-range airliner, but with 368 passengers on board, it ould not reach New Zealand. It would have to land at orfolk Island, between New Zealand and Australia.

LIFE ON THE WING

Most swifts rarely land between leaving their nest for the first time and building their own nest 2–4 years later. They mate, eat, and sleep in flight. It is not known how much ground they cover in that time.

New Zealand

After spending 8 days in the air, and with the fat in its 450-g (1-lb) body almost used up, the godwit arrives in its wintering grounds in a river estuary in New Zealand.

How **old** is the **oldest tree?**

The world's **oldest living tree** started life in around 3050 BCE, making it more than **5,065 years old.** The tree is a **Great Basin bristlecone pine** in the White Mountains of California, USA.

1804 First steam locomotive is built

c.800 CE Vikings raid northwest Europe

The **oldest bristlecone pine** has lived through all of **recorded human history.**

432 BCE Parthenon is completed in Greece

OLDEST SEED

While excavating King Herod's Palace at Masada, Israel, in the 1960s, archaeologists found Judean date palm seeds that were at least 2,000 years old. In 2005, one seed successfully sprouted and was planted at Kibbutz Ketura. The tree has been nicknamed "Methuselah" after the Biblical man said to be the oldest person ever to live.

When the world's oldest tree sprouted from its seed, people wrote with pictures and symbols, not letters and words; the wheel was unknown in most of the world; and the great civilization of ancient Egypt was only just beginning.

c.3050 BCE The tree's seed sprouts

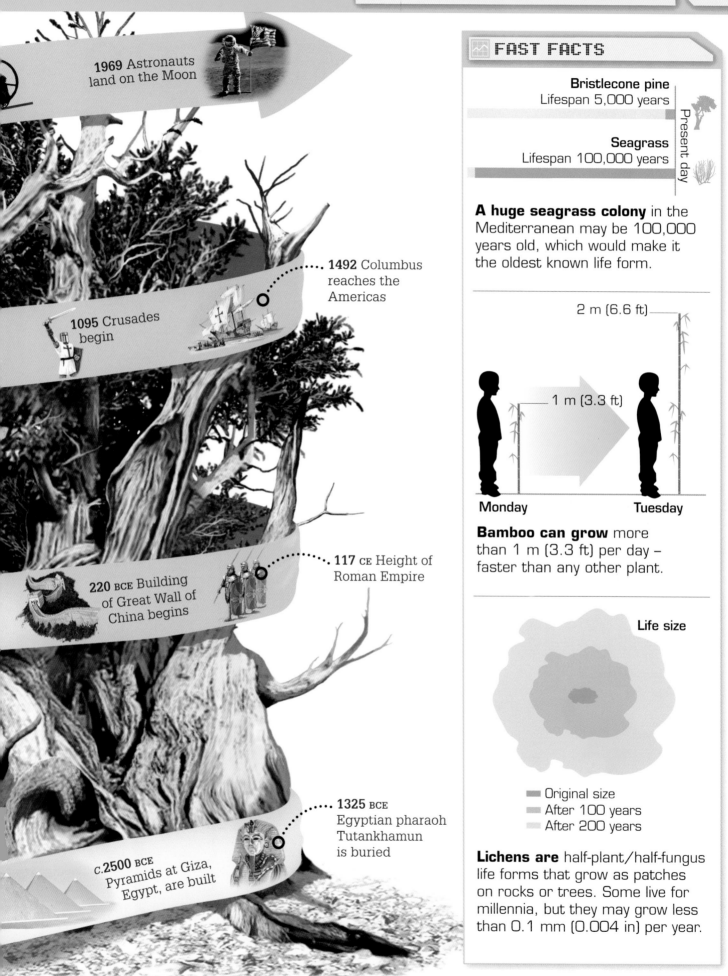

1969 Astronauts land on the Moon

1492 Columbus reaches the Americas

1095 Crusades begin

117 CE Height of Roman Empire

220 BCE Building of Great Wall of China begins

1325 BCE Egyptian pharaoh Tutankhamun is buried

*c.***2500** BCE Pyramids at Giza, Egypt, are built

FAST FACTS

Bristlecone pine
Lifespan 5,000 years

Seagrass
Lifespan 100,000 years

Present day

A huge seagrass colony in the Mediterranean may be 100,000 years old, which would make it the oldest known life form.

2 m (6.6 ft)

1 m (3.3 ft)

Monday

Tuesday

Bamboo can grow more than 1 m (3.3 ft) per day – faster than any other plant.

Life size

Original size
After 100 years
After 200 years

Lichens are half-plant/half-fungus life forms that grow as patches on rocks or trees. Some live for millennia, but they may grow less than 0.1 mm (0.004 in) per year.

How **old** are the oldest animals?

Ocean quahog clams are known to live for more than **500 years.** Scientists think some **sponges** may live **even longer.**

ANCIENT SPONGES

It is difficult to identify the age of a sponge, but Caribbean giant barrel sponges (left) have very long lives; one is believed to be 2,300 years old. Some Antarctic glass sponges may live for more than 10,000 years.

Ocean quahogs can live nearly **6 times longer** than Asian elephants.

Human
122 years

Rougheye rockfish
140–200 years

Most humans don't live 122 years, but there is a verified case of a woman who did.

Asian elephant
86 years

Olm
(a cave salamander)
100 years

Tuatara
111 years

FAST FACTS

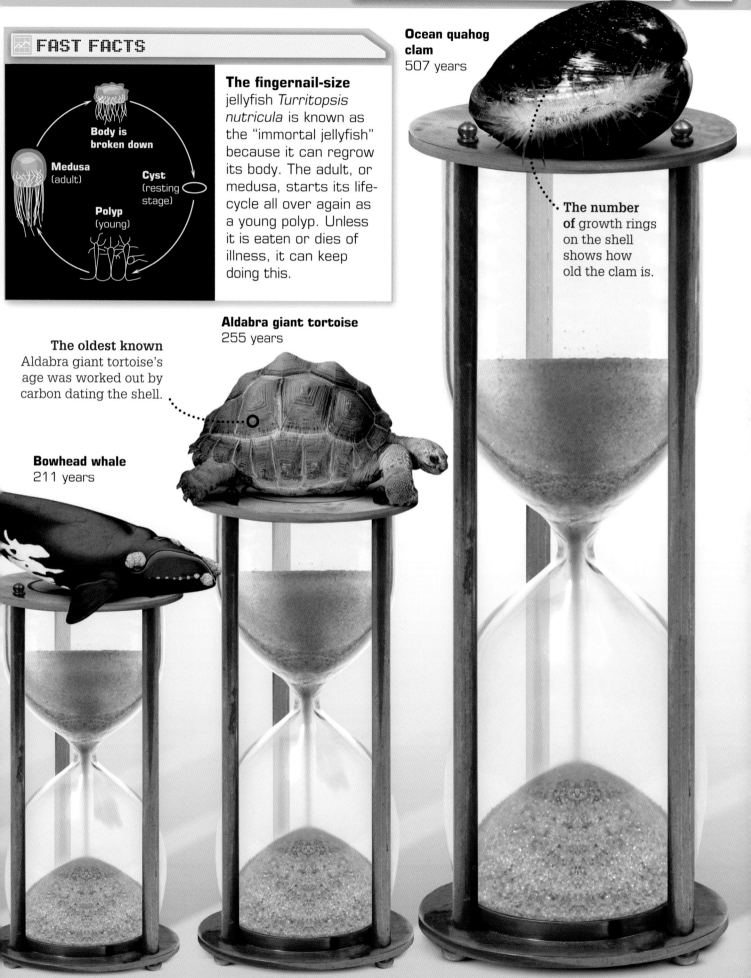

Body is
broken down

Medusa
(adult)

Cyst
(resting
stage)

Polyp
(young)

The fingernail-size jellyfish *Turritopsis nutricula* is known as the "immortal jellyfish" because it can regrow its body. The adult, or medusa, starts its life-cycle all over again as a young polyp. Unless it is eaten or dies of illness, it can keep doing this.

Ocean quahog clam
507 years

The number of growth rings on the shell shows how old the clam is.

Aldabra giant tortoise
255 years

The oldest known Aldabra giant tortoise's age was worked out by carbon dating the shell.

Bowhead whale
211 years

Life-form data

LIFE ON EARTH

Mammals, birds, reptiles, amphibians, and fish are all **vertebrates** (animals with a backbone). Together they make up just **3 per cent** of all animal species. **Invertebrates** (animals without a backbone) make up the remaining **97 per cent**.

VERTEBRATES **3%**

INVERTEBRATES **97%**

Nearly one quarter of all the animal species named so far are **beetles**, amounting to around **400,000 species**. In contrast, fewer than 6,000 mammal species have been identified.

THE BIG ONES

The biggest land animals tower over the average human being.

MAN **1.8 M (6 FT)**

BIGGEST BIRD OSTRICH **2.75 M (9 FT)**

BIGGEST LAND ANIMAL ELEPHANT **4 M (13 FT)**

TALLEST LAND ANIMAL GIRAFFE **6 M (20 FT)**

BIRDS IN FLIGHT

A bird's **wing-shape** depends on the **way it flies**. Birds that live in open areas have **long wings** suited to **gliding** and **soaring**. Birds that live in dense vegetation have **shorter wings** good for flying in **quick bursts**.

SPEED FLYING
Long, thin wings slip easily through the air

QUICK TAKE-OFF
Short, powerful wings flap fast

GLIDING
Long wings catch sea winds and allow bird to glide effortlessly

SAFETY IN NUMBERS

In 1889, a swarm of locusts with an area of **5,000 sq km** (2,000 sq miles) crossed the Red Sea in the Middle East. It is estimated to have weighed around **450,000 tonnes** (500,000 tons) and contained **250 billion locusts**.

The **African red-billed quelea** is the **most numerous** wild bird species on the planet and forms gigantic flocks.

There are 1.5 billion breeding pairs.

Termite colonies can contain up to

3 million

individuals. The **largest termite mound** ever discovered was

12.8 m

(42 ft) tall.

Argentine ants live in giant groups known as **mega-colonies**. One of the **largest** is believed to stretch for

6,000 km (3,700 miles)

along Europe's Mediterranean coast.

MICRO WORLD

A single gram of soil can contain **40 million bacteria**.

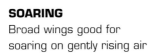

SOARING
Broad wings good for soaring on gently rising air

RAPID MANOEUVRES
Short, curved wings allow quick direction changes

TREES AND PLANTS

The **tallest trees** in the world are the **coast redwoods** of California, USA. The tallest recorded specimen, named Hyperion, stands more than **115 m** (380 ft) high – the height of almost two and a half Statues of Liberty.

COAST REDWOOD **HYPERION 115 M** (380 FT)

Some species of kelp can grow up to **30 cm** (12 in) in a single day.

The rare Southeast Asian plant *Rafflesia arnoldii* (also known as the corpse flower) has the world's

largest, and possibly smelliest, flower. It measures around **1 m** (39 in) across and stinks of rotting flesh.

The smallest flowering plant is *Wolffia globosa*. It measures just **0.6 mm** (0.02 in) long and **0.3 mm** (0.01 in) wide.

WOLFFIA (ACTUAL SIZE)

GIANT KELP

What is the fastest runner?

The fastest sprinters, running the 100 m in less than 10 seconds, reach their top speed usually during the 60–80 m stretch. If they could sustain this top speed throughout the race, they would run it in 8.4 seconds.

43 kph (27 mph)

The **cheetah** is the **fastest land animal**, but only over short distances. **Horses** are **slower**, but can run **much further** before they get tired.

WALKING ON WATER

Basilisk lizards can escape from predators by running across the surface of ponds and rivers. Running at a speed of around 6 kph (4 mph), they can cover a distance of 20 m (65 ft) before they start to sink.

At its **top speed**, a **cheetah** would **finish** a **100 m sprint** in around **3 seconds**.

A thoroughbred racehorse can gallop at up to 70 kph (43 mph) in races of 2 furlongs (0.4 km, 0.25 miles). Running at this speed, the horse could complete the 100 m sprint in 5.15 seconds.

70 kph (43 mph)

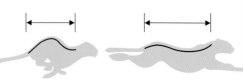

FAST FACTS

The cheetah's speed comes from its flexible spine. The cat hunches its spine at the start of a stride, bringing its back feet in front of the forefeet. As the back feet hit the ground and push off, its spine extends, giving the cheetah an extra-long stride.

Snail 0.05 (0.03)
Mouse 13 (8)
Squirrel 21 (13)
Elephant 40 (25)
Human 43 (27)
Domestic cat 48 (30)
Greyhound 69 (43)
African lion 89 (55)
Pronghorn 100 (62)

Top speed in kph (mph)

The garden snail certainly takes its time to move around. However, the domestic cat is quite fast – it could beat an Olympic sprinter if it had to make a run for it.

115 kph (70 mph)

A cheetah can sprint at incredible speeds to catch its prey, but the chase will only last for about 30–60 seconds, after which the cat gets too tired.

What animal can **jump** the furthest?

GLIDING MAMMALS

Some animals do not jump but can glide for long distances. For example, the sugar glider of Australia, uses flaps of skin between its limbs to help it glide from tree to tree for 50 m (160 ft) of more.

The **snow leopard** of central Asia can **leap further** than any other animal. It can cover more than **15 m** (50 ft) in a **single jump**.

9 m (30 ft)

8.95 m (29 ft 4.5 in)

3 m (9 ft)

The jerboa's long back legs help it to jump more than 25 times its body length.

FAST FACTS

The flea is the most impressive jumping creature on the planet for its size. Fleas can be only 1.5 mm (0.06 in) long but can leap a distance of 33 cm (13 in) – 220 times their body length. Fleas are parasites and spring onto mammals, sometimes including humans, to feed on their blood.

If a flea were the size of a 1.8-m (5-ft 11-in) human, and if it were still able to leap 220 times its own body length, it could clear more than three football pitches laid end to end.

When it jumps, the red kangaroo can reach a speed of more than 64 kph (40 mph) with single leaps of up to 9 m (30 ft).

The human world record for men's long jump was set by US athlete Mike Powell in 1991.

15 m (50 ft)

The **snow leopard** could easily clear **seven large family cars** in one leap.

Snow leopards live in mountain habitats where they leap to catch their prey of wild sheep and goats.

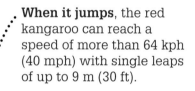

What is the fastest flyer?

In level flight, a **white-throated needletail** is the **fastest** bird in the air. It has a **top speed** of **170 kph** (105 mph).

The white-throated needletail is a species of swift. These birds spend most of their time high in the sky hunting for insects and rarely land. Needletails travel long distances, breeding in Siberia, China, and Japan, then migrating south to countries such as Australia.

DIVING SPEEDS

The peregrine falcon has the fastest dive of any bird. It flies up high, looking for prey. When it spots a duck or a pigeon, it folds its wings and drops into a steep dive at speeds some estimate at more than 300 kph (186 mph). At the last minute it stretches out its talons to snatch its victim.

FAST FACTS

Although they walk with a slow waddle, ducks and waders are the fastest flying birds, other than swifts, that have been measured accurately. The great snipe has the fastest recorded migration.

Common swift
111 kph (69 mph)

Great snipe (a wader)
97 kph (60 mph)

Eider duck
76 kph (47 mph)

Birds are the fastest fliers, but among other animals, free-tailed bats are the quickest. Dragonflies are among the speediest insects.

Mexican free-tailed bat
64 kph (40 mph)

Flying fish
60 kph (37 mph)

Dragonfly
50 kph (30 mph)

A white-throated needletail flies fast enough to keep up with a high-speed train.

Long, curved wings slip easily through the air.

This high-speed train has a maximum speed of 200 kph (125 mph) but on a scheduled passenger journey, it averages about 171 kph (106 mph), including stops.

What is the fastest swimmer?

The **speediest swimmer**, the **sailfish**, could travel the length of an Olympic **swimming pool** in **1.6 seconds** – around **13 times faster** than the **human** record holder.

📈 FAST FACTS

Sailfish
110 kph (68 mph)

Striped marlin
80 kph (50 mph)

Blue-fin tuna
71 kph (44 mph)

Blue shark
69 kph (43 mph)

Swordfish
64 kph (40 mph)

Dall's porpoise
56 kph (35 mph)

California sea lion
40 kph (25 mph)

Octopus
40 kph (25 mph)

Gentoo penguin
36 kph (22 mph)

Leatherback turtle
35 kph (21.5 mph)

The fastest swimmers are all fish. At the top is the sailfish, which is an amazing 30 kph (18.5 mph) quicker than its nearest rival, the striped marlin.

Some other sea animals swim fast. However, all are slower than the top five fastest fish, which have perfectly streamlined bodies with powerful muscles built for speed.

8.6 kph
(5.3 mph)

An Olympic swimmer can keep up his top sprint speed for only one length of the pool (50 m, 164 ft).

Polar bears can swim very long distances. Scientists tracked one bear over a 675-km (420-mile) journey. It took nearly 10 days, and the bear didn't stop to eat or sleep.

108 kph
(67 mph)

The fastest jet-skis can zoom across the water at about 12.5 times the speed of the Olympic swimmer.

A sailfish can dart through water at **110 kph (68 mph), faster than a jet-ski**.

110 kph
(68 mph)

A sailfish is a predator of the open ocean. It uses its speed and large dorsal fin to herd a shoal of fish into a ball. It then slashes its prey with its long bill.

How deep can animals go?

Some animals, such as **sea urchins**, can live at a depth of **10 km** (7 miles), at the bottom of **ocean trenches.** Even **air-breathing** animals, which must hold their breath, can **dive** to **2,388 m** (7,835 ft).

LIVING LIGHTS

The deep-sea anglerfish has a fleshy rod growing from its head with a light on the end. In the complete darkness of the deep ocean, this glowing bait lures small fish and shrimp into the predator's gaping jaws.

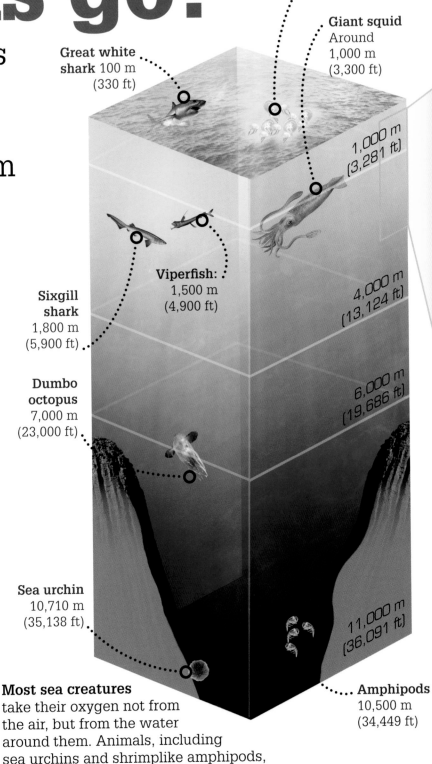

Box jellyfish 0.3–4 m (1–13 ft) deep

Giant squid Around 1,000 m (3,300 ft)

Great white shark 100 m (330 ft)

1,000 m (3,281 ft)

Viperfish: 1,500 m (4,900 ft)

Sixgill shark 1,800 m (5,900 ft)

4,000 m (13,124 ft)

Dumbo octopus 7,000 m (23,000 ft)

6,000 m (19,686 ft)

Sea urchin 10,710 m (35,138 ft)

11,000 m (36,091 ft)

Amphipods 10,500 m (34,449 ft)

Most sea creatures take their oxygen not from the air, but from the water around them. Animals, including sea urchins and shrimplike amphipods, can live in the deepest parts of the ocean.

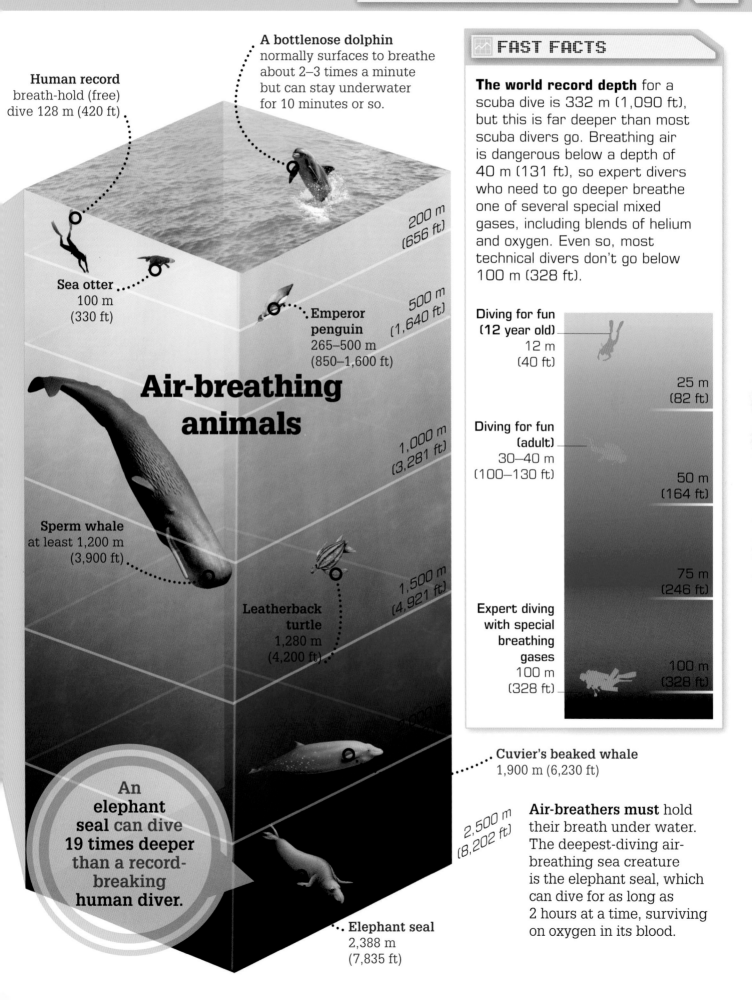

Human record
breath-hold (free)
dive 128 m (420 ft)

A bottlenose dolphin
normally surfaces to breathe
about 2–3 times a minute
but can stay underwater
for 10 minutes or so.

Sea otter
100 m
(330 ft)

200 m
(656 ft)

**Emperor
penguin**
265–500 m
(850–1,600 ft)

500 m
(1,640 ft)

Air-breathing
animals

1,000 m
(3,281 ft)

Sperm whale
at least 1,200 m
(3,900 ft)

**Leatherback
turtle**
1,280 m
(4,200 ft)

1,500 m
(4,921 ft)

**An
elephant
seal can dive
19 times deeper
than a record-
breaking
human diver.**

Cuvier's beaked whale
1,900 m (6,230 ft)

2,500 m
(8,202 ft)

Elephant seal
2,388 m
(7,835 ft)

FAST FACTS

The world record depth for a
scuba dive is 332 m (1,090 ft),
but this is far deeper than most
scuba divers go. Breathing air
is dangerous below a depth of
40 m (131 ft), so expert divers
who need to go deeper breathe
one of several special mixed
gases, including blends of helium
and oxygen. Even so, most
technical divers don't go below
100 m (328 ft).

**Diving for fun
(12 year old)**
12 m
(40 ft)

25 m
(82 ft)

**Diving for fun
(adult)**
30–40 m
(100–130 ft)

50 m
(164 ft)

75 m
(246 ft)

**Expert diving
with special
breathing
gases**
100 m
(328 ft)

100 m
(328 ft)

Air-breathers must hold
their breath under water.
The deepest-diving air-
breathing sea creature
is the elephant seal, which
can dive for as long as
2 hours at a time, surviving
on oxygen in its blood.

How strong is an ant?

An **average-sized ant**, weighing about **0.003 g** (0.0001 oz), is able to **carry an object** that weighs **0.15 g** (0.005 oz) – that's **50 times** its **own weight.**

If a **man** were as **strong as an ant**, he would be able to **lift three cars.**

An ant carries objects in its mandibles – powerful jaws that it also uses to cut, crush, fight, and dig.

This leaf-cutter ant is 0.75 cm (0.3 in) long and can carry a piece of bark much larger than itself.

LEOPARD STRENGTH

When a leopard kills large prey, such as an antelope, it drags the body up a tree, away from hyenas and other scavengers. A male leopard can drag prey three times its weight – even a small giraffe – to a height of 6 m (20 ft).

Ants are strong because their muscles are bigger relative to the ant's overall size. Physics explains that an ant twice as long would have muscles four times stronger, but a body eight times heavier. This would make the muscles – and the ant – effectively half as strong.

If a man weighing 80 kg (176 lbs) could lift 50 times his own weight, that would be 4 tonnes (4.4 tons) – around the same as three cars.

FAST FACTS

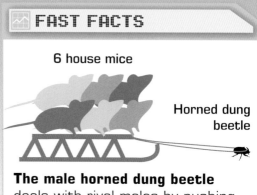

6 house mice

Horned dung beetle

The male horned dung beetle deals with rival males by pushing them out of its burrow. Tests have shown that this species can pull 1,141 times its own body weight – the same as pulling six 20-g (0.7-oz) house mice.

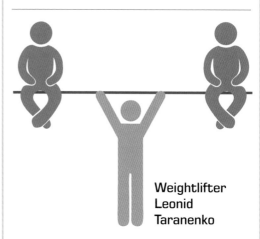

Weightlifter Leonid Taranenko

The largest weight lifted by a human is 266 kg (586 lb). This was achieved by Leonid Taranenko of Russia in 1988 and was nearly twice his body weight. The women's weight-lifting record belongs to Tatiana Kashirina of Russia, who lifted 193 kg (425.5 lb) in 2014.

Animal data

L O N G MIGRATIONS

9,700 KM
(6,000 MILES)

Leatherback turtles regularly swim **9,700 km** (6,000 miles) each way across the Pacific Ocean between their main feeding sites in California and their breeding areas in Indonesia.

5,000–7,000 KM
(3,000–4,500 MILES)

Eels in Europe have to travel **5,000–7,000 km** (3,000–4,500 miles) to their breeding grounds in the Sargasso Sea.

3,200 KM
(2,000 MILES)

Each year, **monarch butterflies** fly on average **3,200 km** (2,000 miles) between southern California and Mexico.

BIG MIGRATIONS

Every year on Africa's Serengeti Plains more than **1.5 million wildebeest** undertake a **2,900-km** (1,800-mile) round trip on the search for fresh grass. Around **250,000**, or **17%**, don't survive.

17%

Africa's biggest migration takes place each autumn when around **8 million fruit bats** fly from the Democratic Republic of the Congo to neighbouring Zambia to feast on newly ripened fruit.

SENSITIVE ANIMALS

▶ **Great white sharks** can detect blood in the water from up to **5 km** (3 miles) away. It's been estimated that they can smell a **single drop of blood in**

100 litres

(26 gallons) of water.

▶ **Jewel beetles** have an infrared sensor that allowing them to **detect a forest fire** from up to **80 km** (50 miles) away. They then fly

towards the fire

and lay their eggs in the burnt tree trunks.

▶ **Seals** have the most sensitive whiskers of any mammal and can **detect a fish** swimming more than **100 m** (330 ft) away.

▶ The heat sensitive organs of **pit vipers** can detect **temperature** variations of just

0.002°C

(0.001°F).

FLYING FISH

Flying fish can soar over the water for up to **200 m** (655 ft) – the length of two average football pitches.

KILLER CREATURES

▶ The sting of a **box jellyfish** is nearly always fatal unless treated immediately. Stings have killed more than **5,500 people** in the past 60 years.

▶ The venom of a **king cobra** can kill an adult human in **15–30 minutes**.

▶ A drop of venom from the **marbled cone snail** can kill **20 humans**, or one elephant.

FASTEST FLAPPERS

Some species of **hummingbird** can flap their wings at up to **80 times a second** – so *fast* it produces a faint humming sound.

HOW SNAKES MOVE

All snakes slide along the ground, but not all move in quite the same way. They have a few main ways of getting around on land:

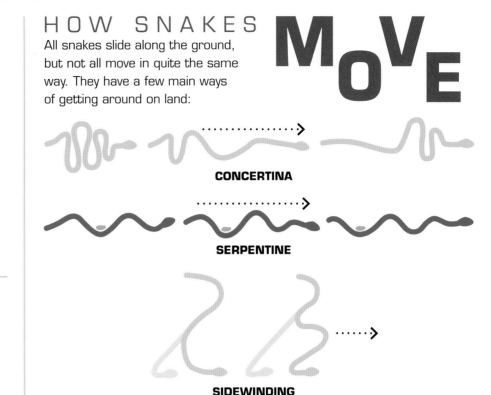

CONCERTINA

SERPENTINE

SIDEWINDING

SLOWEST ANIMALS

While a **cheetah** may be able to race at up to **110 kph** (70 mph), some other creatures prefer to take their time getting from A to B.

SEAHORSE
0.015 KPH
(0.01 MPH)

GIANT TORTOISE
0.3 KPH
(0.2 MPH)

GARDEN SNAIL
0.05 KPH
(0.03 MPH)

6 M (20 FT)

200 M (655 FT)

They can stay in the air for up to **45 seconds**, travelling at around **60 kph** (37 mph) and reaching heights of **6 m** (20 ft).

Feats of engineering

People are inventive and are always creating new things. Engineering – designing and making things – has given us powerful rockets, super-fast sports cars, spectacularly tall buildings, computers that can do billions of calculations per second – and much more.

One of the greatest engineering feats ever, Dubai's Palm Islands are the biggest manmade islands in the world. Palm Jumeirah (pictured) is shaped like an enormous palm tree, covering an area of 5 sq km (3.1 sq miles) – more than the area of 800 football pitches.

How **fast** is the **fastest car?**

The **fastest cars** in **motor sport** are **top fuel dragsters**, which reach **530 kph** (330 mph) from a **standing start** in less than **4 seconds.**

185 kph (115 mph)

372.6 kph (231.5 mph)

A family car, such as this Ford Focus, can barely go half as fast as a Formula 1 car.

The highest speed during a Formula 1 race was set by Juan Pablo Montoya during the 2005 Italian Grand Prix.

AMERICAN COMPETITOR

The Hennessey Venom GT is chasing Bugatti's top road-car spot. It holds a world record of 13.63 seconds for acceleration from 0–300 kph (0–186 mph). It has also reached a speed of 428 kph (266 mph), which is only slightly behind its German rival.

431.1 kph (267.8 mph)

FAST FACTS

Wind-powered
Ecotricity Greenbird 202.9 kph (126.1 mph)

Production road car
Bugatti Veyron 431.1 kph (267.8 mph)

Motorcycle
Ack Attack 605.7 kph (376.4 mph)

Wheel-driven
Vesco Turbinator 756.7 kph (470.3 mph)

Jet-propelled
Thrust SSC 1,228 kph (763 mph)

The fastest cars of all are those designed to beat the world land speed record. During record attempts, cars are timed over two straight-line runs. Jet- and rocket-powered cars have held the main record since the 1960s, but other records exist for different types of vehicle, such as wind-powered.

"Top fuel" is a class of car used in drag racing. These cars run on a mix of special, high-performance fuels and race on a strip that is only 300 or 402 m (1,000 or 1,320 ft) long. They can accelerate from 0–160 kph (0–100 mph) in less than a second, and have to release parachutes behind them to help them brake.

530 kph (330 mph)

The **fastest dragster** reaches speeds **160 kph (100 mph) greater** than any **Formula 1 car.**

The Bugatti Veyron Super Sport is the fastest production car — that is one built in numbers for people to drive on the road. It can accelerate from 0–100 kph (0–62 mph) in 2.46 seconds. It is built by a German-owned French company.

The *Shanghai Maglev* covers 30 km (18½ miles) in less than 8 minutes.

STEAM POWER

The first trains were powered by steam. The fastest of all time was the *Mallard*, a British locomotive that reached 203 kph (126 mph).

FAST FACTS

The fastest maglev train speeds have been reached by Japan's maglev test train, the *MLX01*. A manned rocket sled, however, has achieved even faster speeds.

Rocket sled
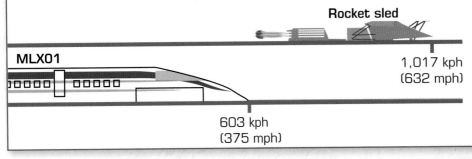

1,017 kph (632 mph)

MLX01

603 kph (375 mph)

270 kph (168 mph)

The yellow *TGV La Poste* is the world's fastest freight train. It is used to transport mail in and out of Paris, France.

How **fast** is the **fastest train?**

The *Shanghai Maglev* is the **fastest passenger train** in the world. It can operate at speeds of up to **430 kph** (267 mph).

China's *Shanghai Maglev Train* is the fastest passenger train in service. Maglevs run on special tracks that lift them off the ground. They are smoother and quieter than ordinary trains.

320 kph (200 mph)

430 kph (267 mph)

The French *TGV* is the world's fastest wheel-based passenger train. It runs on high-speed tracks at up to 320 kph (200 mph) on regular services. A specially adapted version, the *TGV V150*, currently holds the world speed record of 575 kph (357 mph).

The track is called a guideway. When an electric current is sent through the guideway, magnets under the train generate a force that lifts and propels the train at high speed.

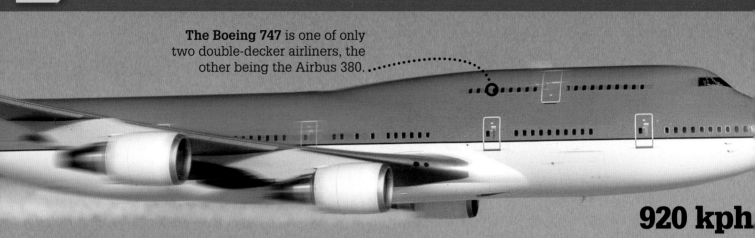

The Boeing 747 is one of only two double-decker airliners, the other being the Airbus 380.

920 kph
(572 mph)

Although more than 40 years old, the Boeing 747 is typical of today's large jet airliners, which fly passengers at an average speed of 877 kph (545 mph) to a top speed of 920 kph (572 mph).

Concorde was the fastest ever passenger jet. It was capable of flying from New York to London in less than 3 hours.

2,179 kph
(1,354 mph)

How **fast** is the **fastest aircraft?**

The **X-15** was the fastest **manned aeroplane** ever to fly. Its **record speed** of **7,297 kph** (4,534 mph) was set in **1967** and has never been beaten.

FAST FACTS

Flyer
48 kph
(30 mph)

Mallard duck
105 kph (65 mph)

The first aircraft to fly, the Wright brothers' *Flyer*, reached a top speed of 48 kph (30 mph). This is less than half the speed of a mallard duck, which flies at 105 kph (65 mph).

7,297 kph (4,534 mph)
X-15 – fastest manned aircraft

4,184 kph (2,600 mph)
SpaceShipTwo – fastest passenger spaceplane

3,529 kph (2,193 mph)
SR–71 Blackbird – fastest jet aircraft

1,126 kph (700 mph)
Cessna Citation X – fastest passenger jet

400 kph (249 mph)
Westland Lynx – fastest helicopter

The fastest aircraft fly to the edge of space. Tourists may soon travel there in supersonic spaceplanes.

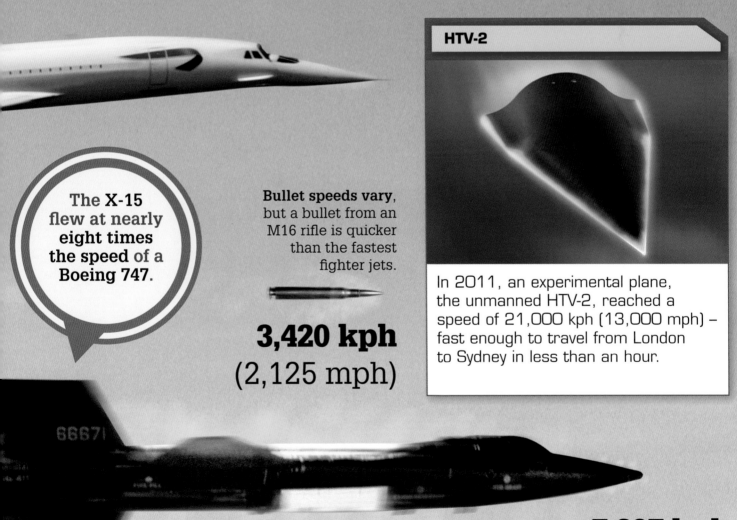

HTV-2

The X-15 flew at nearly eight times the speed of a Boeing 747.

Bullet speeds vary, but a bullet from an M16 rifle is quicker than the fastest fighter jets.

3,420 kph
(2,125 mph)

In 2011, an experimental plane, the unmanned HTV-2, reached a speed of 21,000 kph (13,000 mph) – fast enough to travel from London to Sydney in less than an hour.

The X-15 couldn't take off like an ordinary plane. The experimental aircraft was carried by a bomber to its cruising altitude. Only then did the X-15 fire up its rocket engines.

7,297 kph
(4,534 mph)

The **LZ-130** *Graf Zeppelin II* could carry up to 72 passengers, plus a 40-man crew. With a top speed of 131 kph (81 mph), it had a range of 16,500 km (10,250 miles). The airship was filled with lighter-than-air gas and built to carry passengers across the Atlantic.

The **biggest Zeppelins** were **3 times longer** and **6 times wider** than a Jumbo Jet.

AIRBUS BELUGA

The Airbus Beluga is designed to carry large or awkwardly shaped cargo. This includes the parts for Airbus airliners, which are made in four different countries and then airlifted for assembly.

The control gondola contained separate control and observation rooms, plus a central navigation area.

Huge windows, which could be opened during flights, ran the length of the passenger decks.

What was the biggest aircraft?

At **245 m** (804 ft) **long**, the **Zeppelin airships** *Graf Zeppelin II* and *Hindenburg*, built in Germany in the 1930s, were the **largest aircraft** ever to take to the skies.

The Boeing 747-400D, launched in 1991, can carry up to 600 passengers, compared to the 72-person capacity of *Graf Zeppelin II*.

Each of the four engine cars were manned by a mechanic at all times during flights.

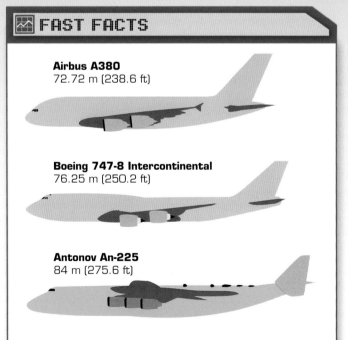

📈 **FAST FACTS**

Airbus A380
72.72 m (238.6 ft)

Boeing 747-8 Intercontinental
76.25 m (250.2 ft)

Antonov An-225
84 m (275.6 ft)

The Antonov An-225 is the world's longest aeroplane – longer than the Airbus 380 and the Boeing 747. Designed to carry *Buran*, the Russian Space Shuttle, on its back, it now finds work transporting outsized cargo items.

How fast is the fastest watercraft?

A record of **511 kph** (318 mph) was set by a **speedboat**, the *Spirit of Australia*, in 1978. It has yet to be beaten.

The *Spirit of Australia* is five times faster than *Hydroptère*.

📊 FAST FACTS

Sometimes you can go almost as fast on a board as you can on a boat. The kitesurfing record of 103 kph (64 mph) is close behind the fastest sailing craft, *Sailrocket 2*, and is faster than *Hydroptére's* 95 kph (59 mph). The fastest windsurfer is nearly as fast.

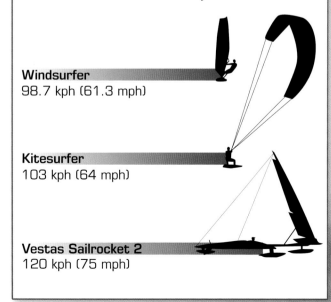

Windsurfer
98.7 kph (61.3 mph)

Kitesurfer
103 kph (64 mph)

Vestas Sailrocket 2
120 kph (75 mph)

Under each side float of *Hydroptère* is a foil, or wing. Once the boat is at a certain speed, the foils lift it so that it almost flies above the water.

The Jet Ski's small size, fast speed, and ease of use make it ideal for use by police, life guards, and fun seekers.

108 kph (67 mph)

Hydroptère was one of the fastest sailing vessels ever made. The boat was built for speed and its crew aimed to break sailing world speed records.

Hydroptère

95 kph (59 mph)

The Spirit of Australia was a jet-powered speed boat driven by Australian Ken Warby.

SPIRIT OF AUSTRALIA
THE WORLDS FASTEST BOAT

FOSSEYS

KW2N

511 kph (318 mph)

📈 FAST FACTS

Harmony of the Seas
362 m (1,187 ft)

Knock Nevis
458 m (1,504 ft)

USS Enterprise (aircraft carrier)
342 m (1,123 ft)

Azzam
180 m (590 ft)

Statue of Liberty
93 m (305 ft)

The longest supertanker ever was the *Knock Nevis*, which was broken up in 2010. The USS *Enterprise* is the longest naval ship in the world, but it is still shorter than the largest cruise ship, the *Harmony of the Seas*. The *Harmony* is nearly as tall as the Statue of Liberty, and twice the length of the *Azzam*, the largest private yacht.

How **big** is a supertanker?

The *TI Oceania* is the same length as 29 US school buses placed end to end.

The *Oceania* and its three sister ships are the largest ever oil tankers to have double hulls – the bottom and sides of the ship have two watertight walls to prevent oil spills in the event of an accident.

The anchor from the *Knock Nevis* weighed 36 tonnes (40 tons) — more than seven African bull elephants. It is the only part of the ship that remains.

HARMONY OF THE SEAS

The world's biggest cruise ship, the *Harmony of the Seas,* can carry up to 5,479 passengers and 2,100 crew. Cruise ships are like floating towns with restaurants, cinemas, shops, and swimming pools. The *Harmony* even has a full-size basketball court!

At **380 m** (1,246 ft) **long** and **68 m** (223 ft) **wide**, the *TI Oceania* is the **biggest supertanker** afloat today. It can carry **3 million barrels of oil**, and when full weighs **441,585 tonnes** (486,764 tons).

TI Oceania **has** a top speed of 16.5 knots (31 kph/19 mph). At this speed it would take 46 seconds for the entire ship to pass someone watching from the shore.

TI OCEANIA

Protective red paint indicates the area of the hull that lies below the water when the supertanker is fully laden.

How much can a ship carry?

The **biggest container ship**, *MSC Oscar*, can carry **19,224** standard size **containers**. It is **395.4 m** (1,297 ft) **long**.

The bridge (from where the captain controls the ship) sits far forward so containers ca be stacked high without the captain losing visibil

Standard containers are used to transport all kinds of goods all over the world, from fruit to clothes and TVs. Each standard container is 6.1 m (20 ft) long and 2.44 m (8 ft) wide, and can be lifted from the ship to fit directly onto a lorry or train.

📊 FAST FACTS

The biggest tankers can carry even more cargo than container ships. The *Knock Nevis* supertanker was 458 m (1,504 ft) long and could hold 4.1 million barrels of oil — enough to fill 260 Olympic swimming pools.

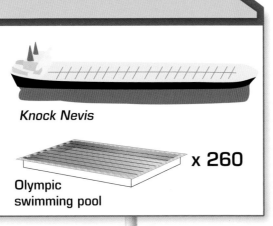

Knock Nevis

x 260

Olympic swimming pool

Heavy-lift ships, such as the *Blue Marlin*, transport huge structures such as oil rigs or aircraft carriers. The ship can submerge its deck to duck under the structure, then raise it again once the cargo has been loaded.

If every container were fully loaded, the boat would be too heavy to sail. It can carry a maximum 197,362 tonnes (217,554 tons), or 10 tonnes (11 tons) per container.

At 73 m (240 ft) tall, the *MSC Oscar* is as tall as a 25-storey building. It is also 13 times longer than a blue whale, and seven buses could park end-to-end across its 59-m (194-ft) width. It sails between Asia and Europe.

MSC OSCAR

Fully loaded, *MSC Oscar* could carry 38,448 cars or 920 million tins of soup.

How **powerful** was the **Space Shuttle?**

The **Shuttle's** three engines and two rocket boosters produced **3.1 million kg** (6.8 million lb) of **thrust**.

Fuel tank full of liquid hydrogen and liquid oxygen.

Two solid rocket boosters provided 71 per cent of the thrust needed for lift-off.

USA

The temperature inside the Shuttle's engines reached 3,315°C (6,000°F).

FAST FACTS

The Space Shuttle's three engines could burn the equivalent of 2.4 swimming pools of liquid fuel in a minute – that's 3,785 litres (1,000 gallons) a second.

Swimming pool
10 x 6 m (33 x 20 ft)

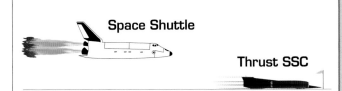

Space Shuttle

Thrust SSC

The Space Shuttle took just under 40 seconds to reach a speed of 1,000 kph (621 mph). However, the holder of the world land speed record, the *Thrust SSC* rocket car, reached this speed in 16 seconds – less than half the time taken by the Shuttle.

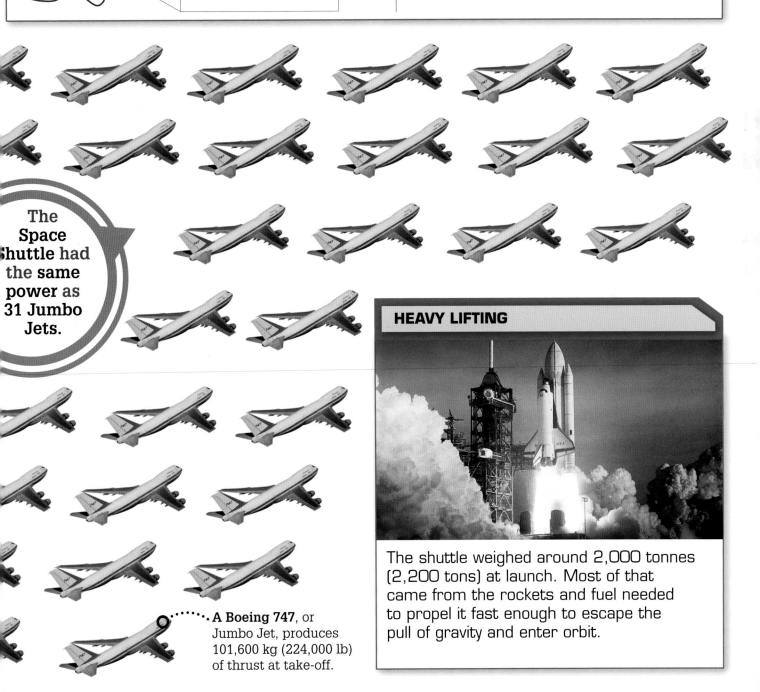

The Space Shuttle had the same power as 31 Jumbo Jets.

HEAVY LIFTING

The shuttle weighed around 2,000 tonnes (2,200 tons) at launch. Most of that came from the rockets and fuel needed to propel it fast enough to escape the pull of gravity and enter orbit.

A Boeing 747, or Jumbo Jet, produces 101,600 kg (224,000 lb) of thrust at take-off.

How **far** have **people** been into **space?**

In **1970**, the crew members of the **Apollo 13 Moon mission** travelled a record distance of **400,171 km (248,655 miles) from Earth.**

3. A few hours before splashdown, the Service Module was detached and the crew saw for the first time the huge damage that had been caused by the explosion.

4. The Command Module re-entered Earth's atmosphere at a speed of 39,733 kph (24,689 mph).

The Lunar Module is the part of the spacecraft designed to detach in Moon orbit and descend to the Moon's surface.

The Command Module is where the crew sits during the journey to the Moon.

The Service Module contained a rocket motor, fuel, oxygen, and the electrical power supply.

📊 FAST FACTS

Voyager 1 is the farthest-flung human-built object in space. It is 20 billion km (12.4 billion miles) from Earth, and in 2012 became the first craft to leave our Solar System.

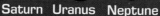

Solar System

Saturn   Uranus   Neptune   Pluto

Earth °   Distance
Solar System distances are measured in AU (Astronomical Units). One AU is the distance between Earth and the Sun.

Apollo 13's mission was to orbit the Moon 111 km (69 miles) from its surface, travelling the same distance as previous Apollo Moon missions. Some crew members were going to land on the Moon's surface. When an explosion disabled the spacecraft, however, the mission changed. The spacecraft had to be sent on a new, longer path around the Moon, just to get the crew home safely.

2. Apollo 13 flew 264 km (164 mi) past the Moon before swinging back on its return path.

The **distance from Earth reached by Apollo 13 is equivalent to 10 circuits of Earth's equator**.

1. The craft was 329,000 km (204,000 miles) from Earth and 55 hours into its flight when an explosion crippled the Service Module's fuel, power, and oxygen supplies. The mission to land on the Moon had to be aborted.

MISSION CONTROL

In the Apollo 13 Service Module, a fan in an oxygen tank short-circuited, causing the tank to catch fire and explode. Mission controllers on Earth worked out that they could use the Moon's gravity to bring the craft back on course for home.

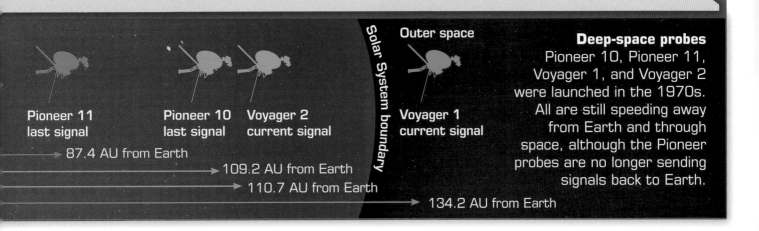

Pioneer 11
last signal

Pioneer 10
last signal

Voyager 2
current signal

Solar System boundary

Outer space

Voyager 1
current signal

Deep-space probes
Pioneer 10, Pioneer 11, Voyager 1, and Voyager 2 were launched in the 1970s. All are still speeding away from Earth and through space, although the Pioneer probes are no longer sending signals back to Earth.

87.4 AU from Earth

109.2 AU from Earth

110.7 AU from Earth

134.2 AU from Earth

How high was the highest parachute jump?

In 2012, Austrian **Felix Baumgartner leapt** from a balloon nearly **39,000 m** (128,000 ft) above the Earth.

At the edge of space, the air pressure is less than 2 per cent of what it is at sea level. Baumgartner wore a pressurized suit to prevent himself from blacking out as he fell.

Wispy cirrus clouds can form as high as 14,000 m (46,000 ft).

The **skydive** was roughly **four times** the **height of** a crusing airliner.

Airliners usually cruise at around 10,000 m (33,000 ft).

Most parachute jumps are made from less than 4,300 m (14,100 ft). Even at this height, you will freefall at around 160 kph (100 mph).

BREAKING THE SOUND BARRIER

During freefall Baumgartner reached a speed of 1,358 kph (844 mph), becoming the first person to break the sound barrier without the help of a vehicle.

Baumgartner travelled
to a height of 38,969 m
(127,852 ft) in a balloon
before jumping from
the capsule.

Jumping from the stratosphere is
very risky. The air is far too thin to
breath, but Baumgartner could only
carry a 10-minute supply of air with
him for the descent. The lack of air
pressure also made it hard to stop
himself spinning as he fell. Luckily
he managed to pull himself into a
proper freefall position.

FAST FACTS

Only rocket planes are able
to fly high in the atmosphere
because the lack of oxygen
prevents jet engines working.

The stratosphere lies
above the troposphere,
to an altitude of
50,000 m (160,000 ft).

**International
Space Station**
354,000 m
(1,161,400 ft)

The troposphere,
the lowest layer
of the atmosphere
where most cloud
and weather occurs,
ends at 12,000 m
(40,000 ft).

At 33,500 m
(110,000 ft)
Baumgartner
broke the
sound barrier.

**Passenger spacecraft
SpaceShipTwo**
110,000 m
(359,000 ft)

**Highest rocket
aeroplane X-15**
108,000 m
(354,200 ft)

**Highest jet
aeroplane
SR-71 Blackbird**
24,000 m
(80,000 ft)

At 1,500 m (4,900 ft)
above the ground,
Baumgartner opened his
parachute and landed
safely on the ground.

Passenger airliner
10,000 m (33,000 ft)

Transport data

ON AND **ON** AND **ON**

A Volvo car built in 1966 had by 2012 driven

4.7 million km

(2.9 million miles) — that's the equivalent of almost **117 times** around the globe.

WORLD'S
BIGGEST

Tunnel boring machine
With a diameter of **19.25 m** (63 ft) and a weight of **3,800 tonnes** (4,200 tons), this mighty machine is being used to dig a new road tunnel beneath St Petersburg, Russia.

Propeller
Measuring **10.3 m** (33.8 ft) across and weighing **102.5 tonnes** (113 tons), this giant propeller was built in Germany and transported to South Korea.

DOWN DEEP

332 m (1,090 ft) Deepest scuba dive

610 m (2,001 ft) Deepest dive in an atmospheric diving suit

490 m (1,608 ft) Operating depth of the nuclear submarine USS Seawolf

4,500 m (14,800 ft) Maximum diving depth of the US Navy manned submersible Alvin

Deepsea Challenger

Trieste

11,030 m (36,200 ft) Challenger Deep, the deepest point, has been visited twice: in 1960 by the submersible *Trieste*; and in 2012 by *Deepsea Challenger*.

LONGEST NON-STOP PASSENGER FLIGHTS

15 HOURS, 25 MINUTES

Sydney, Australia to Dallas-Fort Worth, USA: **13,804 km** (8,577 miles)

17 HOURS, 15 MINUTES

Auckland, New Zealand to Dubai: **14,203 km** (8,825 miles)

LONGEST TRAIN

- The world's longest train had **682 cars** and eight locomotives. It was used just once, to haul iron ore in Australia in 2001, and it measured **7.353 km** (4.57 miles) long. That's the length of **8.8 Burj Khalifas**, laid end to end.

- The longest ever passenger train ran in Australia in 2004. It was **1.2 km** (0.75 miles) long and was made up of two locomotives and **43 carriages**.

TOTAL AMOUNT OF RAILWAY TRACK IN THE WORLD

More than **1,239,615 km** (770,262 miles) — more than three times the distance from Earth to the Moon.

The three countries with the most railway track are the USA, China, and Russia. Between them they have just under one third of all the world's track.

USA: **224,792 km** (139,679 miles)

China: **121,000 km** (75,186 miles)

Russia: **86,000 km** (53,400 miles)

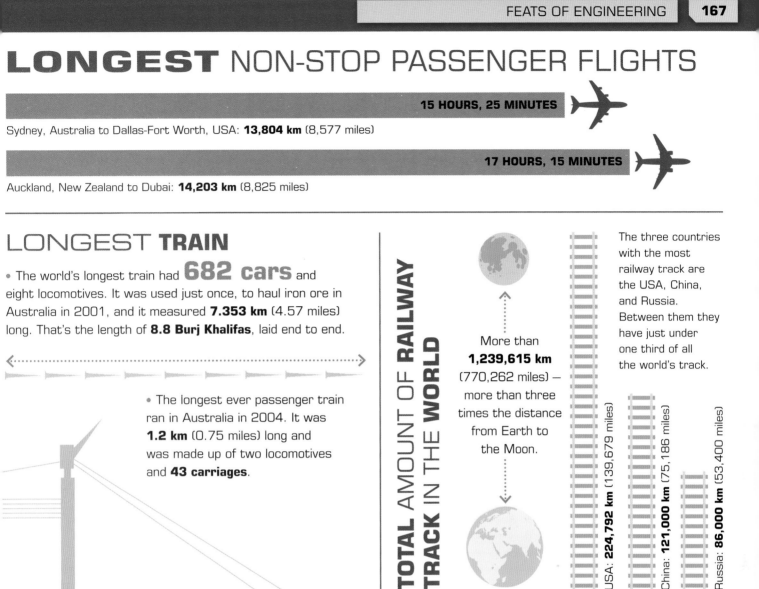

Land vehicle

An enormous excavator used in the German mining industry, the **Bagger 293** is **225 m** (738 ft) long, **96 m** (315 ft) high and weighs **14,200 tonnes** (15,652 tons). It can fill 2,400 coal wagons a day.

Human

Animal
The blue whale measures **30 m** (100 ft) long.

How **small** is the **tiniest** computer?

A **miniscule computer** less than the size of a grain of rice can **read temperatures**, **take pictures**, and **record pressure readings**. It is small enough to be **injected into the body** or to **detect pockets of oil** in rock.

📈 FAST FACTS

Computers are getting smaller each year. In 1993, to do 143 GFLOPS (143 billion calculations a second) you needed a computer 1.5 m (5 ft) tall and 8 m (25 ft) long. Only 20 years later, just four laptops exceeded this performance.

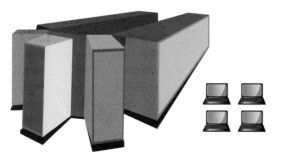

Intel Paragon supercomputer, 143 GFLOPS

4 Intel i5 laptop processors, 45 GFLOPS each

Moore's Law, invented by Gordon Moore, a founder of Intel, suggests that computers double in perfomance every two years. In fact, the average speed of the 500 fastest computers in the world more than doubled every two years during the decade 2002–2012.

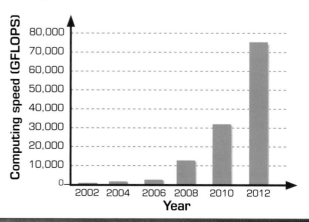

This miniature device, called the Michigan Micro Mote, could have lots of different uses. As well as being inserted into the body to measure temperature or pressure, or used to find oil, it could also help us avoid losing things in our homes. Sticking the tiny computers onto keys or wallets could help us find these items using a central system.

The computer doesn't have a battery, but uses light as a source of power. It doesn't need to be natural sunlight, so the computer can work indoors.

It would take about 150 of these computers to fill a thimble.

MICROPROCESSORS

Computers became a lot smaller in 1971 with the invention of the microprocessor — the silicon chip that is the central processing unit of a computer. A silicon chip has a miniature electrical circuit printed on it. These printed circuits are smaller every year.

How many books can you fit on a flash drive?

A **1-terabyte (TB)** flash drive can store the text of **1 million books**. One terabyte is just over **1 million megabytes** (MB), or more than **1 trillion bytes**.

A flash drive weighs less than 30 g (1.1 oz) but can hold 1 TB of data. Flash memory can be erased and reprogrammed thousands of times.

A **1-TB** flash drive could store **1 million 200-page** books.

ATOMIC DATA STORAGE

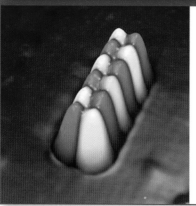

Seen here under a powerful electron microscope is the world's smallest data storage unit. Scientists have used just 12 iron atoms to hold one bit (the basic unit of information), and 96 atoms to hold a byte. A hard disk still needs half a billion atoms per byte.

FAST FACTS

The Library of Congress in Washington DC is the biggest library in the world, containing 35 million books. All the text in those books could be stored on nine 4-TB hard disks.

36-TB

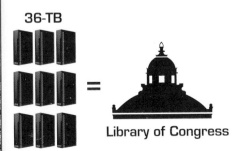

= Library of Congress

Storage media are getting more sophisticated every few years. Each piece of new technology stores many times more data than the previous one. They are also becoming faster and, because they have no moving parts, smaller and more durable.

**3.5"
floppy disk**
1.44 MB

Zip disk
100 MB

CD
700 MB

DVD
4.7 GB

**Dual-layer
Blu-ray disk**
50 GB

**2-TB Flash
drive**
2 TB

Computer data

SOCIAL **NETWORKS**

In 2007, fewer than **500 million** people around the world used social networking sites, such as Facebook. Over the next 5 years, this figure grew to more than

1.2 BILLION — more than

82% of the world's online population.

VIDEO GAME DEVELOPMENT
COST$

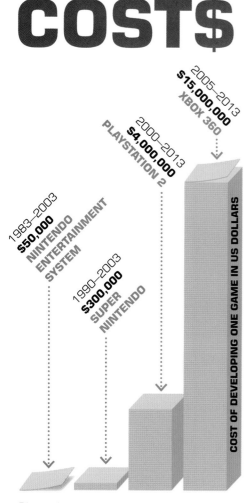

2005–2013
$15,000,000
XBOX 360

2000–2013
$4,000,000
PLAYSTATION 2

1983–2003
$50,000
NINTENDO ENTERTAINMENT SYSTEM

1990–2003
$300,000
SUPER NINTENDO

COST OF DEVELOPING ONE GAME IN US DOLLARS

Since the early 1980s, the **average cost of developing a video game** has increased by more than

30,000%.

COMPUTER MEMORY
GROWTH

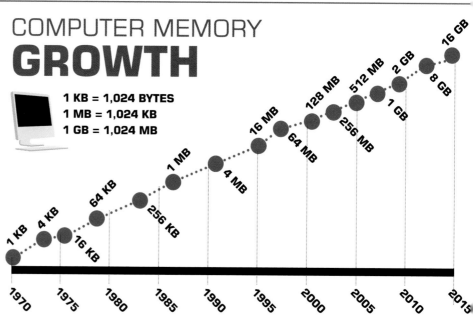

1 KB = 1,024 BYTES
1 MB = 1,024 KB
1 GB = 1,024 MB

1 KB • 4 KB • 16 KB • 64 KB • 256 KB • 1 MB • 4 MB • 16 MB • 64 MB • 128 MB • 256 MB • 512 MB • 1 GB • 2 GB • 8 GB • 16 GB

1970 1975 1980 1985 1990 1995 2000 2005 2010 2015

SUPER
COMPUTER

The world's **fastest computer**, the **Tianhe-2**, uses **8,000 kW** of electricity when it is running at full speed. That's equivalent to **1 million** energy-saving 8-watt **light bulbs**.

PERCENTAGE OF **PEOPLE ONLINE** IN EACH CONTINENT IN 20

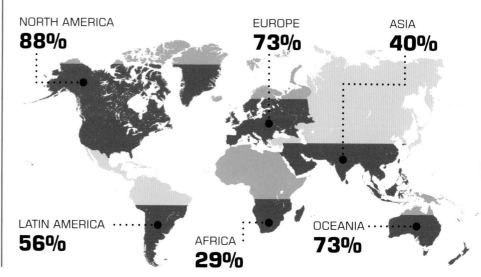

NORTH AMERICA **88%**

EUROPE **73%**

ASIA **40%**

LATIN AMERICA **56%**

AFRICA **29%**

OCEANIA **73%**

FLOOR SPACE

ENIAC, the world's **first electronic computer**, was built in 1946. It covered **167 sq m** (1,798 sq ft), and could perform **10,000** calculations per second. **Today's fastest computer, Tianhe-2**, covers **720 sq m** (7,750 sq ft), and performs **33,860 trillion** calculations per second.

MOON LANDING

The **computer** onboard the **Apollo 11** spacecraft that landed on the Moon in 1969 had just **72 kb** of memory, of which just **2 kb** was RAM.

WEBSITE GROWTH

Since 1991, the number of websites has grown from 1 to more than 1 billion.

,000,000,000

700,000,000

600,000,000

500,000,000

400,000,000

300,000,000

200,000,000

FIRST WEBSITE:
http://info.cern.ch
6 August 1991

100,000,000

0

1990   1995   2000   2005   2010   2016

@ YOU'VE GOT MAIL

The **first email** was sent by computer engineer Ray Tomlinson in Cambridge, Massachusetts, USA, in **1971**.

E-BOOK GROWTH

Percentage of book sales in the USA, the world's biggest book market, that were e-books

2002:	**0.05%**	2009:	**3.17%**
2006:	**0.50%**	2011:	**16.97%**
2008:	**1.18%**	2012:	**22.55%**

In 2012, online booksellers reported that e-books were outselling paper books for the first time.

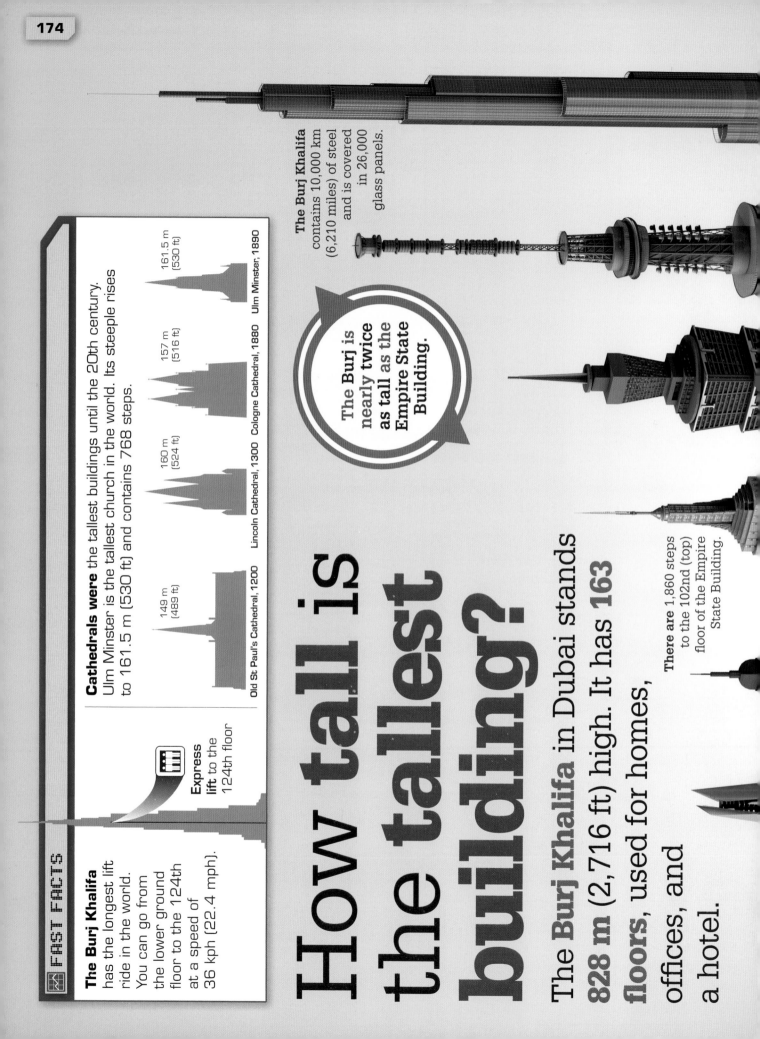

How tall is the tallest building?

The **Burj Khalifa** in Dubai stands **828 m (2,716 ft)** high. It has **163 floors**, used for homes, offices, and a hotel.

There are 1,860 steps to the 102nd (top) floor of the Empire State Building.

The Burj is nearly twice as tall as the Empire State Building.

The Burj Khalifa contains 10,000 km (6,210 miles) of steel and is covered in 26,000 glass panels.

The Burj Khalifa has the longest lift ride in the world. You can go from the lower ground floor to the 124th at a speed of 36 kph (22.4 mph).

Express lift to the 124th floor

Cathedrals were the tallest buildings until the 20th century. Ulm Minster is the tallest church in the world. Its steeple rises to 161.5 m (530 ft) and contains 768 steps.

149 m (489 ft)
Old St Paul's Cathedral, 1200

160 m (524 ft)
Lincoln Cathedral, 1300

157 m (516 ft)
Cologne Cathedral, 1880

161.5 m (530 ft)
Ulm Minster, 1890

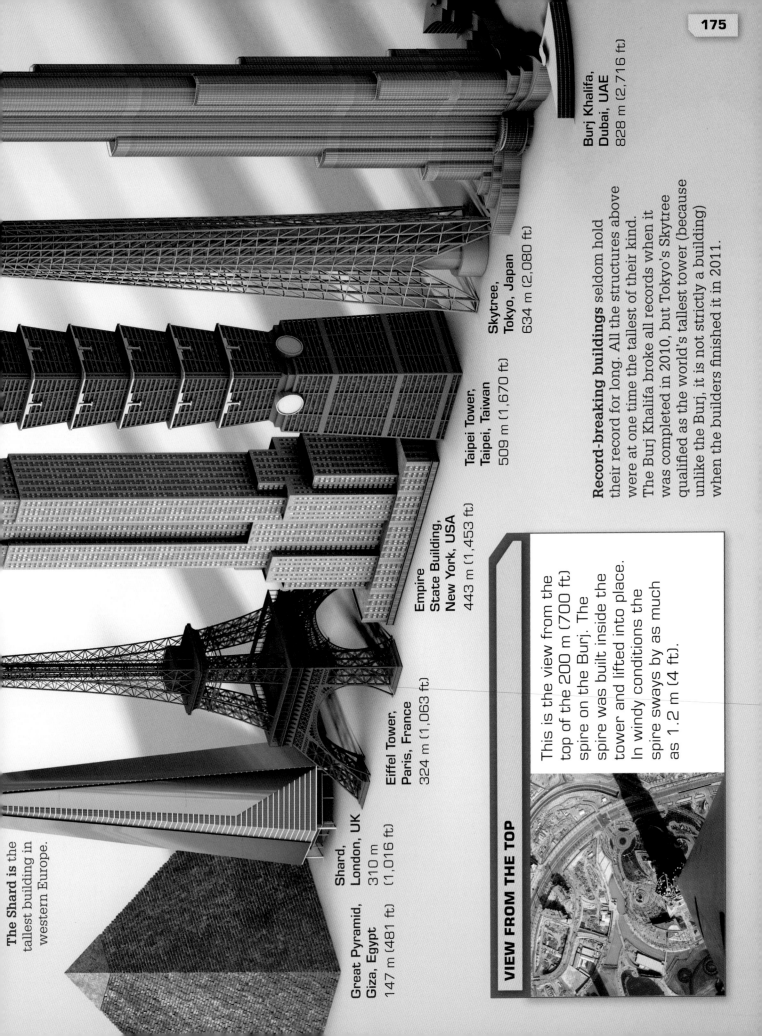

The Shard is the tallest building in western Europe.

Great Pyramid,
Giza, Egypt
147 m (481 ft)

Shard,
London, UK
310 m
(1,016 ft)

Eiffel Tower,
Paris, France
324 m (1,063 ft)

Empire
State Building,
New York, USA
443 m (1,453 ft)

Taipei Tower,
Taipei, Taiwan
509 m (1,670 ft)

Skytree,
Tokyo, Japan
634 m (2,080 ft)

Burj Khalifa,
Dubai, UAE
828 m (2,716 ft)

Record-breaking buildings seldom hold their record for long. All the structures above were at one time the tallest of their kind. The Burj Khalifa broke all records when it was completed in 2010, but Tokyo's Skytree qualified as the world's tallest tower (because unlike the Burj, it is not strictly a building) when the builders finished it in 2011.

VIEW FROM THE TOP

This is the view from the top of the 200 m (700 ft) spire on the Burj. The spire was built inside the tower and lifted into place. In windy conditions the spire sways by as much as 1.2 m (4 ft).

Around the top of the roof of the London stadium, the lighting towers reach 60 m (197 ft) above the sports area.

You could fit 3 London Olympic stadiums inside the factory walls.

The Boeing 747 is 19 m (64 ft) high and was the biggest aircraft in the world when the factory was built in the 1960s.

How **big** is the **biggest building?**

A huge mural on the side of the building covers six doors, each of which is 25 m (82 ft) high and the length of a National Football League (NFL) field.

Used for putting aeroplanes together, **Boeing's Everett Factory** in Seattle, USA, has a **volume** of **13.4 million cu m** (472 million cu ft).

The **Everett factory is** so huge you could fit the whole of Disneyland or 55 soccer pitches inside. Beneath the plant are 3.7 km (2.33 miles) of pedestrian tunnels.

PRODUCTION LINE

This single bay inside the plant is holding 12 aeroplanes waiting to be painted. The Everett factory can produce eight Boeing 777s and ten 787s a month.

The perimeter of the building measures 3.5 km (2.2 miles).

FAST FACTS

About 600 litres (160 gallons) of paint are applied to each Boeing 747 – that is 7.5 bathfuls.

The Everett Factory is the biggest building by volume, but others have a larger floor space.

Everett Factory, Seattle
398,000 sq m
(4.28 million sq ft)

Pentagon, Washington
610,000 sq m
(6.6 million sq ft)

Abraj Al-Bait Towers hotel, Mecca:
1.6 million sq m (17 million sq ft)

Dubai International Airport,
Terminal 3: 1.71 million sq m
(18.4 million sq ft)

FAST FACTS

Millau bridge deck
36,000 tonnes
(40,000 tons)

**5 x
Eiffel Towers**

The bridge's steel deck contains enough to steel to make five Eiffel towers. The deck was built in a total of 2,200 separate sections which were welded together into two halves, then pushed out towards each other from opposite sides of the valley.

Each of the longest cables on the viaduct is strong enough to withstand the thrust of eight Boeing 747 airliners at maximum thrust.

How tall is the tallest bridge?

The Millau Viaduct carries the road from Montpellier, in southern France, to Paris. The bridge is 2,460 m (8,070 ft) long and was opened in 2004.

The **Millau Viaduct**, which spans the valley of the river **Tarn** in **France**, is the **tallest bridge** in the world. Its **largest mast** is **343 m** (1,125 ft) above the base, where it meets the **valley floor**.

The tallest mast is 343 m (1,125 ft) tall. There are seven masts of different heights across the valley. Each holds 11 pairs of stays (metal cables). The stays support the road deck.

The Empire State Building measures 381 m (1,250 ft) to its roof. If it sat in the bottom of the valley, the roof would be just 12 m (40 ft) above the bridge's highest point.

LONGEST BRIDGE

The world's longest bridge is the Danyang–Kunshan Grand Bridge in China at 164.8 km (102.4 mi) long. The bridge is part of the Beijing–Shanghai High-Speed Railway. Two more of the world's five longest bridges are part of the same railway line.

The Millau Viaduct is almost as tall as the Empire State Building.

How much gold is there?

From **ancient times** to the **present day**, experts estimate that just **171,300 tonnes** (188,800 tons) of **gold** have been dug out of the ground.

GOLD NUGGETS

A nugget is a naturally occurring lump of gold. Most nuggets are small – but not all of them. This top shelf shows a model of the Welcome Stranger nugget, found in Australia in 1869 and weighing about 78 kg (173 lb).

A tennis court is 23.78 m (78 ft) long. ⋯⋯

A ball the width of a tennis court might not sound big enough for 171,300 tonnes (188,800 tons) of gold, but gold is a very heavy metal. Two solid gold house bricks would weigh as much as an adult person.

The ball may look like a lot of gold, but this is all the gold that has ever been mined anywhere on Earth, since the beginning of history. Every day, the world produces enough iron to make more than 40 iron balls of the same size!

All the world's **mined gold** would make a **solid ball 24 m** (78.7 ft) **across.**

FAST FACTS

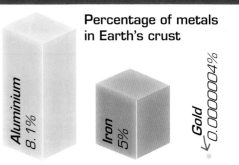

Percentage of metals in Earth's crust

Aluminium 8.1%

Iron 5%

Gold 0.0000004%

Gold is much rarer than iron or aluminium, which make up large percentages of Earth's crust. Gold is valuable because it is so rare, but also because its shiny beauty never rusts or tarnishes.

Gold left in the ground

Mined Gold

We have already mined about 80 per cent of the world's recoverable gold. Only 46,000 tonnes (51,000 tons) of the gold left in the ground could be extracted with existing technology.

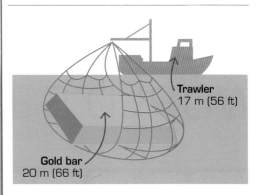

Trawler 17 m (56 ft)

Gold bar 20 m (66 ft)

Sea water contains dissolved gold. There may be up to 15,000 tonnes (16,500 tons) of it in the world's oceans. If this gold could be extracted, it would make a bar measuring 20 m x 10 m x 4 m (66 ft x 33 ft x 13 ft).

ACKNOWLEDGEMENTS

Dorling Kindersley would like to thank: Neha Gupta and Samira Sood for proofreading, Helen Peters for indexing, Fran Baines, Carron Brown, Matilda Gollon, Caroline Stamps and Fleur Star for editorial assistance; Rachael Grady, Mary Sandberg, Jemma Westing, and Jeongeun Yule Park for design assistance; and Simon Holland, Katie John, Martyn Page, and Chris Woodford, for fact checking.

The publisher would like to thank the following for their kind permission to reproduce their photographs:

(Key: a-above; b-below/bottom; c-centre; f-far; l-left; r-right; t-top)

2 Corbis: STScI / NASA (tr). 3 Corbis: National Geographic Society / Richard Nowitz (tl); Michele Westmorland (tc). Dreamstime.com: Pictac (bl); Haider Yousuf (tr). 4-5 Corbis: STScI / NASA. 6-7 Alan Friedman / avertedimagination.com: (c). 6 Institute for Solar Physics: SST / Göran Scharmer / Mats Löfdahl (bl); 7 NASA: GSFC / F. Espenak (cl/Reproduced five times). 8 NASA: Hinode / XRT (clb). 9 Dreamstime.com: Elisanth (cra/ Reproduced four times, cr/ moons); Stanalin (tr, crb, cr). 10-11 Pascal Henry,www.lesud.com. 10 NASA: (clb). 12-13 Pascal Henry,www.lesud.com: (c). 13 NASA: JPL / Space Science Institute (tc). 14-15 Science Photo Library: Mark Garlick. 14 Dorling Kindersley: London Planetarium (fcl). Dreamstime.com: Elisanth (cl). 15 NASA: (bc). 16 Dreamstime.com: Mmeeds (clb). 18 NASA: ESA and H. Hammel, MIT (clb). 20 Dreamstime.com: Jabiru (bl). 25 NASA: ESA, J. Hester, A. Loll (ASU) (tl). 27 NASA: CXC / SAO / F.Seward (tc). 29 NASA Goddard Space Flight Center: Tom Zagwodzki (tr). 31 Corbis: Visuals Unlimited (cr). 32 NASA: (bl). 32-33 Science Photo Library: Chris Butler (c). 33 ESA / Hubble: S. Beckwith (STScI) and the HUDF Team (br). Getty Images: Azem Ramadani (tl). Science Photo Library: Mark Garlick (cr). 36-37 Corbis: National Geographic Society /

Richard Nowitz. 40 Science Photo Library: Geoeye (bc). 43 NASA: Visible Earth / Jeff Schmaltz (cr). 45 Dreamstime.com: Asdf_1 (tc). 46 Dreamstime.com: Ericsch (bl). 48 Dreamstime.com: Maxwell De Araújo Rodrigues (cla/Reproduced seven times). 49 Getty Images: National Geographic (cr). 50 Corbis: Galen Rowell (bl). 52 NASA: JPL / University of Arizona (clb). 54 Corbis: Arctic-Images (clb). 56 Corbis: Charles & Josette Lenars (bc). 57 Getty Images: Mike Copeland (crb). 58-59 Getty Images: National Geographic. 60 Corbis: Paul Souders (clb). 62 Corbis: Science Faction / Norbert Wu (clb). 65 Corbis: Nippon News / Aflo / Newspaper / Mainichi (clb). 66 Getty Images: Paul Souders (bl). 68 NSIDC: USGS, W.O. Field (1941) and B.F. Molnia (2004) (clb). 69 Dreamstime.com: Maxwell De Araújo Rodrigues (cr/ Reproduced five times). 72 Getty Images: Katsumasa Iwasawa (clb). 72-73 Dreamstime.com: Stockshoppe (c). 73 Dreamstime. com: Laraslk (crb). 74 Corbis: Visuals Unlimited (clb). 75 Dreamstime.com: Pictac (bc). 78 Getty Images: (bl). 78-79 Getty Images: Hulton Archive. 80 Corbis: epa / Michael Reynolds (bl). 82 Corbis: Ocean (clb). 82-83 Corbis: Ikon Images / Jurgen Ziewe (c). 84-85 Corbis: Michele Westmorland. 86 Corbis: TempSport / Jerome Prevost (cl). Dreamstime.com: Alexandr Mitiuc (clb, bc, br). 86-87 Dorling Kindersley: Zygote Media Group (c). 87 Dreamstime.com: Alexandr Mitiuc (bl, bc, crb). 88 Getty Images: Vince Michaels (br). Science Photo Library: GJLP / CNRI (clb). 89 Corbis: 3d4Medical.com (bl). 90-91 Alamy Images: D. Hurst. 91 Alamy Images: AlamyCelebrity (tc). 92 Corbis: Science Photo Library / Steve Gschmeissner (cl). 96 Corbis: Visuals Unlimited (clb). 97 Corbis: Minden Pictures / Flip Nicklin (bc). Dorling Kindersley: Natural History Museum, London (bl). 100 Dreamstime.com: Lindsay Douglas (cl). 100-101 National Geographic Stock: Michael Nichols (b). 103 naturepl. com: Doc White (tc). 104 Dorling Kindersley: Bedrock Studios (tc). Dreamstime.com:

Ibrahimyogurtcu (bc). 104-105 Dorling Kindersley: Andrew Kerr (c). 106-107 Dorling Kindersley: Andrew Kerr (c). 107 Dorling Kindersley: Jon Hughes and Russell Gooday (cr). 108 Science Photo Library: Peter Chadwick (clb). 110-111 Science Photo Library: Christian Darkin. 112 Paul Nylander,http://bugman123. com. 113 Alamy Images: Michal Cerny (tc). 114 Alamy Images: Louise Murray (clb). 116-117 Dreamstime.com: Bruce Crandall (c). 118 Alamy Images: Kevin Elsby (t). 119 Alamy Images: Rolf Nussbaumer Photography (bl). Dreamstime.com: Pictac (t). 121 Dorling Kindersley: Natural History Museum, London (tr). Otorohanga Zoological Society (1980): (bl). 124 Dr. Avishai Teicher: (clb). 126 Alaska Fisheries Science Center, NOAA Fisheries Service: (crb). Pearson Asset Library: Lord and Leverett / Pearson Education Ltd (cb). Dreamstime.com: John Anderson (cl); Ispace (fbl, bl, bc, br, fbr). 127 Dreamstime.com: Ispace (bl, bc, br). Photoshot: NHPA / Paul Kay (cra). 130 Getty Images: Jose Luis Pelaez Inc (c); Visuals Unlimited, Inc. / Joe McDonald (clb). 131 Corbis: Minden Pictures / Suzi Eszterhas (c). 132 Corbis: imagebroker / Konrad Wothe (cb). Dreamstime.com: Juri Bizgajmer (b/Reproduced four times). Getty Images: Joe McDonald (cl). 133 Corbis: Wally McNamee (fclb); Robert Harding World Imagery / Thorsten Milse (clb). Dreamstime. com: Juri Bizgajmer (b/ Reproduced three times). Getty Images: Daniel J. Cox (crb). 134 Science Photo Library: Jim Zipp (bc). 134-135 Alamy Images: Matthew Clarke. 136-137 Alamy Images: Transtock Inc. (c). 137 Corbis: Paul Souders (tr). Dreamstime.com: F9photos (tl). Getty Images: Ronald C. Modra (bl). 138 Alamy Images: Bluegreen Pictures / David Shale (clb). Corbis: Wim van Egmond (crb). Dreamstime.com: Ferdericb (ca). naturepl.com: David Shale (cr). 139 Dorling Kindersley: Dolphin Research Center, Grassy Key, Florida, www.dolphins.org (ca); Natural History Museum, London (cl, cb). Getty Images: AFP (cla). 140 Alamy Images:

Duncan Usher (cl). Dreamstime. com: Isselee (br). 141 Dreamstime.com: Georgii Dolgykh (clb); Jezper (tl); Goce Risteski (cl). 144-145 Dreamstime. com: Haider Yousuf. 146 Corbis: epa / ULI DECK (crb); Transtock (clb). Dreamstime.com: Raja Rc (c). Getty Images: Bill Pugliano (cla). 146-147 Corbis: Chris Crisman. 147 Corbis: Icon SMI / J. Neil Prather (c). 148-149 Alstom Transport: P.Sautelet (c). Corbis: Imaginechina (cr). 148 Alamy Images: Sagaphoto.com / Gautier Stephane (c). Getty Images: SSPL (cl). 150 Corbis: George Hall (t). 150-151 Getty Images: Marvin E. Newman (c). 151 Alamy Images: LM (crb). NASA: (b). 152 Alamy Images: DIZ Muenchen GmbH, Sueddeutsche Zeitung Photo (c). Dreamstime.com: Brutusman (clb). 153 Dreamstime.com: Rui Matos (cl). 154-155 Getty Images: AFP / MARCEL MOCHET. 154 Getty Images: Bryn Lennon (b). 157 Dreamstime.com: Richard Koele (b). Alamy Stock Photo: Newzulu (tr). 158 123RF.com: 3ddock (clb). Dreamstime.com: Chernetskiy (b/Reproduced two times). 158-159 A.P. Moller/ Maersk: (c). 159 Dockwise: (tr). 160 Alamy Images: Dennis Hallinan (c). 161 Corbis: Morton Beebe (c/Boeing). NASA: (br). 163 NASA: (cb). 164 Science Photo Library: Ria Novosti (clb). 168-169 Corbis: Science Faction / Louie Psihoyos (finger). 169 University of Michigan: Martin Vloet (c). Alamy Images: David J. Green (crb). 170 Dreamstime.com: Marekp (cb). Sebastian Loth, CFEL Hamburg, Germany: (bl). 175 Getty Images: Barcroft Media / Imre Solt (br). 177 Corbis: Ed Kashi (tr). 178-179 Getty Images: Charles Bowman (c). 179 Getty Images: Edward L. Zhao (tr). 184 Alamy Images: Giffard Stock (clb)

All other images
© Dorling Kindersley

For further information see:
www.dkimages.com